Unlocking the Power of Your QMS

Also available from ASQ Quality Press:

How to Audit the Process-Based QMS
Dennis R. Arter, Charles A. Cianfrani, and John E. (Jack) West

Cracking the Case of ISO 9001:2000 for Manufacturing
Charles A. Cianfrani and John E. (Jack) West)

Cracking the Case of ISO 9001:2000 for Service
Charles A. Cianfrani and John E. (Jack) West

ISO 9001:2000 Explained, Second Edition
Charles A. Cianfrani, Joseph J. Tsiakals, and John E. (Jack) West

The ASQ ISO 9000:2000 Handbook
Charles A. Cianfrani, Joseph J. Tsiakals, and John E. (Jack) West

ISO 9001:2000—An Audio Workshop and Master Slide Presentation,
Second Edition
CD Version
Charles A. Cianfrani and John E. (Jack) West

Certified Quality Manager Handbook, Second Edition
Duke Okes and Russell T. Westcott, editors

From Quality to Business Excellence: A Systems Approach to Management
Charles G. Cobb

The Recipe for Simple Business Improvement
David W. Till

ISO 9001:2000 Aplicada a la Fabricación
Charles A. Cianfrani and John E. (Jack) West

ISO 9001:2000 Aplicada a los Servicios
Charles A. Cianfrani and John E. (Jack) West

To request a complimentary catalog of ASQ Quality Press publications,
call 800-248-1946, or visit our Web site at http://qualitypress.asq.org.

Unlocking the Power of Your QMS

Keys to Performance Improvement

John E. (Jack) West
Charles A. Cianfrani

ASQ Quality Press
Milwaukee, Wisconsin

American Society for Quality, Quality Press, Milwaukee 53203
© 2005 by American Society for Quality
All rights reserved. Published 2004
Printed in the United States of America

12 11 10 09 08 07 06 05 04 03   5 4 3 2 1

Library of Congress Cataloging-in-Publication Data
West, Jack, 1944–
   Unlocking the power of your quality management system : keys to performance
improvement / John E. (Jack) West, Charles A. Cianfrani.
      p. cm.
   Includes bibliographical references and index.
   ISBN 0-87389-592-4 (alk. paper)
   1. Total quality management—Evaluation.   2. Industrial management—
Evaluation.   3. Industrial productivity—Evaluation.   4. Organizational
effectiveness—Evaluation.   5. ISO 9000 Series Standards—Evaluation.
I. Cianfrani, Charles A.   II. Title.

   HD62.15.W465 2004
   658.4'013—dc22   2004015613

ISBN 0-87389-592-4

Publisher: William A. Tony
Acquisitions Editor: Annemieke Hytinen
Project Editor: Paul O'Mara
Production Administrator: Randall Benson
Special Marketing Representative: David Luth

ASQ Mission: The American Society for Quality advances individual,
organizational, and community excellence worldwide through learning, quality
improvement, and knowledge exchange.

Attention Bookstores, Wholesalers, Schools, and Corporations: ASQ Quality Press
books, videotapes, audiotapes, and software are available at quantity discounts with
bulk purchases for business, educational, or instructional use. For information,
please contact ASQ Quality Press at 800-248-1946, or write to ASQ Quality Press,
P.O. Box 3005, Milwaukee, WI 53201-3005.

Quality Press
600 N. Plankinton Avenue
Milwaukee, Wisconsin 53203
Call toll free 800-248-1946
Fax 414-272-1734
www.asq.org
http://qualitypress.asq.org
http://standardsgroup.asq.org
E-mail: authors@asq.org

To place orders or to request a free copy of
the ASQ Quality Press Publications Catalog,
including ASQ membership information,
call 800-248-1946. Visit our Web site at
www.asq.org or http://qualitypress.asq.org.

∞ Printed on acid-free paper

Contents

Acknowledgments

Thanks to family, friends, and colleagues who contributed to the creation of this book.There's always a danger in making specific acknowledgments, because invariably someone very important is not recognized. But we would like to recognize the contributions of San West, Marilyn Cianfrani, Bob Peach, Larry Wilson, Chief Joseph Akpieyi, Craig Johnson, Anna McSorley and Thomas A. Bacus. Your help, support, and encouragement are appreciated.

Introduction

Another book on quality management?

Why?

The intention of this book is to provide insight into how an organization can build on an existing quality management system to make the organization even more successful. Each chapter explains strategies and tactics you could adopt to improve performance through your quality management system. At the end of each chapter is a short section titled "What can I do now?" For each chapter, we suggest formulating a strategy to initiate at least one project to improve the organization. Such a project may be derived directly from the material in the chapter, or it may be a variation of the theme contained in the chapter material. The important point is to do something to improve—NOW.

The book encourages you to consider both the emphasis placed on the various aspects of your organization's quality management system and how results can be enhanced by improving the aspects of the system that you determine are most important.

Quality professionals and executives in organizations with mature fully integrated management systems may be the most enthusiastic readers.

Those who have experienced the improvements that can result from a robust quality management system tend to be encouraged to do more. At the other end of the spectrum, readers who want to expand the breadth and depth of a not yet mature quality management system will also find useful ideas to improve performance.

Although Chapter 1 is a bit heavy, we suggest reading it first. It is a back-to-basics look at the principles upon which quality management is built. The authors have researched these ideas and distilled 12 principles that provide a starting point for organizations to consider when evaluating the integrity of the foundation of a quality management system. In other words, "Does our quality management system address the aspects of quality that are, or will be, fundamental to our success now and for the foreseeable future?"

The remaining chapters can be read in any order. Since most organizations have limitations on resources (both human and capital), we have structured the book in such a way that readers can pick and choose which chapters offer the most significant potential for improvement, perhaps based on a self-assessment (which is addressed in Chapter 9). If a self-assessment has already been conducted, then such an assessment could guide attention to the areas that offer the greatest opportunities for improving performance. Priorities vary by organization, so select those areas for investment that offer your organization the greatest opportunity.

At the end of the book is a short epilogue called Reflections. It calls on the reader to think about what he or she can and should do to lead performance improvement. The authors believe that performance improvement is much too important to be a chance occurrence. It requires a culture where everyone in the organization feels a responsibility to be a "change agent" and feels an obligation to participate in focusing the organization on ensuring its external customers are more satisfied with its products and services than any of its competitors.

We hope this book helps you become a change agent in your organization. Improvement is a never-ending challenge.

1

The Principles Behind Quality Management Systems

"It is often easier to fight for principles than to live up to them."

Adlai Stevenson
Speech in New York City, 1952

Most organizations face extraordinary conditions, including diabolical competitive strategies, daunting regulatory situations, the pressures of "globalization," and dozens of other issues.

Some organizations just get by; they are always fighting fires. While there may be improvements over time, those improvements are often not traceable to the organizations' quality management systems. Because they don't know what caused the improvements, they cannot sustain them or expand upon them.

Other organizations are different. They can point to major improvements in organizational performance that are traceable to actual accomplishments of their quality management systems, processes, and activities. These organizations have developed mature quality management systems that achieve results. Such mature quality management systems have certain characteristics. It is from those characteristics that the principles underlying quality management systems evolved.

The quality management principles are basic ideas or beliefs that have been found to underpin mature quality management systems that have been successful in achieving results. Figure 1.1 gives a working definition of the concept. This chapter discusses what these principles are, the sources from which they were derived, and how they can be used to continually improve performance. The principles can be applied in a minimal or sporadic way in a basic quality management system. The development of a mature quality

Figure 1.1   Principles are fundamental ideas or beliefs on which we can base action.

management system is made easier when the principles are embraced by the organization.

These principles are not new, nor are they revolutionary. Used alone, each may have little impact on organizational performance. When those that are important for an organization are used together, the combination can be a powerful force to guide organizational behavior.

ORIGINS OF THE PRINCIPLES OF ORGANIZATIONAL QUALITY MANAGEMENT

The authors have identified 12 principles that can serve as a foundation of mature quality management systems. They are basic ideas or beliefs that can be used together to form a basis for organizational excellence. The proposed principles were derived from three basic sources:

- The eight quality management principles that appear in ISO 9000:2000[1] and ISO 9004:2000[2] are available on the ISO website. They were used as a basis for the ISO 9000:2000 series, including ISO 9001:2000.[3] The ISO website has a document that "gives the standardized descriptions of the principles as they appear in ISO 9000:2000 and ISO 9004:2000. In addition, it provides examples of the benefits derived from their use and of actions that managers may take in applying the principles to improve their organizations' performance."[4] These principles were developed in a consensus process during the early and mid-1990s. While the thinking on the subject has not changed dramatically since then, these principles do not represent the latest thinking or the impact of current conditions.

- The European Foundation for Quality Management (EFQM) "concepts" are the basis of the European Quality Award. The

1999 version of these concepts was reviewed in 2002 in what was called the Model Refreshing Project. The revised document was issued in 2003. The EFQM report of that review, published on the EFQM Web site stated that the "concepts have largely remained unchanged with the exception of Public Responsibility that becomes Corporate Social Responsibility, a term commonly understood by most organizations." EFQM also says, "The text describing the concepts has been refreshed to make them more vibrant, alive, and understandable. All concepts now have a . . . common start, that is '. . . Excellence is . . .' followed by '. . . some detail of what this may look like and some short bullet point benefits.'"[5] In other words, EFQM has improved a good thing but the basic ideas haven't changed. Presentations on the 2002 model refreshing project and plans for the 2006 version are available for downloading.[6] The current version is available for download from the EFQM website.[7]

- The Malcolm Baldrige National Quality Award (MBNQA) "Core Values and Concepts" form a basis for the Baldrige assessment criteria. Since there is an annual review of the Baldrige criteria, these values and concepts have evolved over time. This makes them somewhat subject to change in order to reflect current buzzwords. It also means the 2004 Core Values may represent the latest thinking. The current version is available for downloading.[8]

The authors also reviewed the 12 quality management principles in the Japanese Standards Association Technical Report Q0005:2003, "Guidelines for Sustainable Growth."[9] This Technical Report was prepared to provide guidance to organizations beyond what is contained in ISO 9004:2000 and emphasizes areas that organizations should consider in order to maintain competitiveness and to achieve sustainable growth.

In early discussions about this chapter, the authors intended to use the eight quality management principles given in the ISO 9000:2000 series without addition or change because they were derived after lengthy study of reference material such as the Baldrige criteria. But the research leading to the eight ISO 9000 principles was done several years ago. And that work reflected a consensus process among experts from a number of countries and several international ballots. In fact, we think that one major concept (a focus on results) was left out. On reflection, it became clear that the business excellence criteria should be reviewed to consider the latest thinking. After this review, the authors decided to expand upon the eight principles of ISO 9000:2000 to include concepts needed for organizations to be successful in the next five years, not the last five. We need to look beyond the ideas in ISO 9000 and the eight principles to embrace newer thinking if we are develop quality management systems today that will remain relevant in the future.

THE 12 PRINCIPLES OF ORGANIZATIONAL QUALITY MANAGEMENT

The result of our review was the formulation of a set of 12 principles. The 12 principles fall into two categories. Seven of them are operational in nature and five are directional. The directional principles provide focus, while the operational ones give a sense of actions that should be taken.

The five directional principles are:

- **Focus on customers**—Customers are the source of both the requirements for products and services and of the revenues that enable an organization's continued existence. Focusing on meeting customers' needs and expectations is therefore essential for organizational survival.

- **Focus on other stakeholders (social responsibility)**—Owners, employees, other interested parties, and society at large may all have a stake in the organization's performance. Focusing on the needs of other stakeholders is important if the organization is to sustain itself.

- **Focus on results**—Organizations need to achieve good results in all key areas of performance to have a viable future. These include results in financial performance, customer satisfaction, quality improvement, environmental performance, and other key areas.

- **Focus on agility**—Being flexible and having rapid response is critical to organizations faced with changing external conditions. This goes beyond achieving operational agility to achieving an organizational mindset that embraces rapid change.

- **Focus on the future**—Focusing on the future helps an organization better manage its own destiny.

Table 1.1 gives the five directional principles and some activities organizations may undertake when they adopt each principle.

Table 1.1 Examples of activities to implement the directional principles.

Principle	Typical activities
Focus on customers—Customers are the source of both the requirements for products and services and of the revenues critical to an organization's continued existence. Focusing on meeting customers' needs and expectations is therefore essential for organizational survival.	• Understand current and future customer needs, wants, and expectations • Measure customer satisfaction and dissatisfaction • Act on customer satisfaction measurement results • Determine, prioritize, and act on things important to customers' buying decisions
Focus on other stakeholders (social responsibility)—Owners, employees, other interested parties, and society at large all have a stake in the organization's performance. Focusing on the needs of other stakeholders is important if the organization is to sustain itself.	• Determine who the key stakeholders are • Measure the needs, wants, and expectations of key stakeholders • Set objectives related to stakeholder needs and act to meet them
Focus on results—Organizations need to achieve good results in all key areas of performance to have a viable future. These include results in financial performance, customer satisfaction, quality improvement, environmental performance, and other key areas.	• Establish a relentless drive to set and meet objectives for quality, customer satisfaction, cost, and other important measurables • Manage processes to achieve objectives for outputs
Focus on agility—Being flexible and having rapid response is critical to organizations faced with changing external conditions. This goes beyond achieving operational agility to achieving an organizational mindset that embraces rapid change.	• Determine external forces that drive the need for agility • Develop a mindset that agility and change are good • Establish objectives for cycle time reduction, flexibility, and speed as needed • Focus on meeting the objectives
Focus on the future—Focusing on the future helps an organization manage its own destiny.	• Establish a long-range planning process • Determine and understand current and needed core competencies • Establish plans to meet future needs

Most organizations will find all five of these items important for their future survival. Some might say if these are the things important to survival, they are the *musts* of the organization. If this were true, all organizations would find each of the five to be of equal importance. It is more common for organizations to find that some are more important than others. For example, in an industry experiencing rapid regulatory changes, focusing on agility may be the key to organizational success. When a single regulatory decision can mean loss of a market, customer requirements could be far less important than being flexible in reacting to regulatory needs. In other cases, it may be most important to focus on customers and meeting their needs.

The seven operational principles are:

- **Provide leadership, vision, and purpose**—Leaders establish the purpose of the organization, its objectives, and its vision of the future. Leaders should build an environment where all members can contribute to meeting the organization's objectives.

- **Establish and align objectives**—Alignment of objectives in all areas of the organization enhances the ability to meet goals and achieve results.

- **Manage a system of interrelated processes**—Managing activities and resources together as a process improves the ability to meet process output needs. Managing the interactions among the processes as a system enables the organization to be more effective and efficient at meeting objectives.

- **Manage with facts supported by credible data**—Decisions should be made using facts and data tempered with experience and intuition.[10]

- **Innovate, learn, and improve**—Organizations achieve excellence by learning, innovating, and improving. It is the people in the organization who are important to learning and innovation.

- **Develop and involve people**—People are the essence of the organization and their full engagement in their work and involvement in improving it helps the organization meet its objectives.

- **Develop suppliers, partners, and other stakeholders**— Active development of suppliers, partners, and other stakeholders helps all create value together.

Table 1.2 gives the seven operational principles and some activities organizations are led to take when they adopt each principle.

Table 1.2   Examples of activities to implement the operational principles.

Principle	Typical activities
Provide leadership, vision, and purpose—Leaders establish the purpose of the organization, its objectives, and its vision of the future. Leaders should build an environment where all members can contribute to meeting the organization's objectives.	• Understand and deploy organizational mission, vision, and core values • Involve all members of the organization in activities to meet organizational objectives • Measure the satisfaction and needs of key stakeholders including members of the organization; act on the results
Establish and align objectives—Alignment of objectives in all areas of the organization enhances the ability to achieve results.	• Understand the full range of customer and key stakeholder requirements • Identify and use key drivers of organizational performance • Develop balanced scorecards to measure progress on key drivers • Make certain each person in the organization knows how he or she contributes to meeting the objectives
Manage a system of interrelated processes—Managing activities and resources together as a process improves the ability to meet process output needs. Managing the interactions among the processes as a system enables the organization to be more effective and efficient at meeting objectives.	• Define a system of processes focused on meeting organizational objectives • Measure process parameters that drive process output results • Use systems thinking to identify, define, and understand process interactions
Manage with facts supported by credible data—Decisions should be made using facts and data tempered with experience and intuition.	• Collect and analyze data related to key drivers • Use data in making decisions, solving problems, and driving improvement
Innovate, learn, and improve—Organizations achieve excellence by continually learning, innovating and improving. It is the people in the organization who are key to learning and innovation.	• Encourage and facilitate learning • Encourage prevention-based activities • Encourage planned innovation at all levels • Drive improvement with performance measurement
Develop and involve people—People are the essence of the organization, and their full engagement in their work and involvement in improving it helps the organization meet its objectives.	• Determine gaps in performance and competence • Provide needed training • Provide feedback to all employees on performance and how they influence organizational objectives
Develop suppliers, partners, and other stakeholders—Active development of suppliers, partners, and other stakeholders helps all create value together.	• Define key partners and the role of each • Help partners develop capabilities • Involve suppliers in determination of customer requirements • Share appropriate information with partners

INTERACTION AMONG
THE 12 PRINCIPLES

Each organization should understand how the 12 principles interact with one another in the organization's own context. Table 1.3 summarizes the nature of these interactions. A brief review of the table indicates that the type and strength of interactions can very well depend on the priorities of each particular organization. If it serves no other purpose, this table should encourage the strategic thinkers in an organization to consider the interrelationships among the principles and the implications of these relationships. Let's look at some simple examples.

Table 1.3   Strength of interrelationships among the principles.

Operational Principles	Directional Principles				
	Customer focus	Focus on other stakeholders (social responsibility)	Focus on results	Focus on agility	Focus on the future
Leadership, vision, and purpose	⌒	⌒	⚡	⌒	⌒
Establish and align objectives	⌒	⌒	⬦	⌒	⌒
Manage a system of interrelated processes	⌒	⌒	⚡	⌒	⌒
Managing with facts supported by credible data	⌒	⌒	⚡	⌒	⌒
Improve, innovate, and learn	⌒	⌒	⚡	⌒	⌒
Develop and involve people	⌒	⌒	⚡	⌒	⌒
Suppliers, partners, and other stakeholders	⌒	⌒	⌒	⌒	⌒

Depends on priorities ⌒   Critical ⚡   Directly related ⬦

A simple business with a simple system and a single realization process may have many competitors and find a close relationship between customer focus and managing the system of processes. In this case, other relationships may be of less relative importance.

A steel fabricating company with a large backlog of work may find a strong relationship between managing the system of processes and achieving results for all stakeholders. This may be the key to future orders.

A company with an aging product line will need to focus on customers to understand and reach its future vision.

It is often easy to find the relationships that are the most important for the near-term success and longer term survival. This is not to say that only the most important relationships should be considered but missing the most important ones will have negative consequences.

MATURITY OF THE QUALITY MANAGEMENT SYSTEM

Organizations can use these principles at varying levels of system maturity. This creates a dilemma that often goes unresolved.

The principles can be applied in a minimal way in a basic quality management system. In such a system, there may be sporadic use of each principle. There may be parts of the organization that embrace them and parts that resist them and their implications.

Quality programs come and go with little linkage between the current program and past efforts. Often, proponents of the latest program criticize the previous one. While progress may be made in the organization, it is often not due to any of these quality initiatives. Such organizations are living with an immature quality management system. Some organizations live in this mode for years.

Organizations with mature quality management systems are quite another matter. Such organizations can point to major improvements in organizational performance. They can directly relate the improved performance to their quality systems, processes, and activities. Some of these quality systems, processes, and activities may have matured in these organizations for years. As we discussed at the beginning of this chapter, organizations with such mature systems have certain characteristics, and it is from those characteristics that the principles evolved.

An organization with a mature quality management system has a broad view of quality. In such organizations, quality is often considered the common denominator by which all things in the organization are managed. And, the quality management system becomes "the way we manage the organization." With this view, we adopt the idea that quality is a variable; there can be good quality, mediocre quality, and bad quality. So, we can have not only high or low quality products in the organization, but we can also have high and low quality earnings, high and low employee morale, high and low environmental performance, and so on. When it comes to products and services, make no mistake about it, customers want good, excellent, or perfect quality. They want their requirements to be met the first time, every time.

DIMENSIONS OF QUALITY MANAGEMENT SYSTEM MATURITY

Quality system maturity has three dimensions:

- **The breadth of the system**—This is how much of the organization's activity is included in the system. A minimum system does not go beyond meeting customer requirements and addressing customer satisfaction. It includes those processes to manage product realization and to ensure customer requirements are met. A mature system is focused on all stakeholders. It includes processes related to meeting the needs of customers, employees, owners, the community at large, the environment, and perhaps other considerations.

- **The depth of the system**—This is how far the system extends up and down the organization. A minimum system may include people involved with meeting customer requirements and leave out everyone else. The mature system includes everyone and all of the organization's processes.

- **The degree of integration**—This is the degree to which the quality processes are integrated into all of the other processes of the organization. Immature quality systems tend to be separate from other activities of the organization. They may involve large quality staffs reporting to a senior manager or a family of stand-alone processes that are carried out by operations personnel. Mature systems are well integrated into the daily work of everyone from the top managers to the lowest level of the organization. While depth and breath may seem intuitive, integration is not. There can be considerable debate about it. Yet it is this dimension that must be managed if the system is to help the organization achieve great things. Integration means one system to manage the organization, not several. It means the

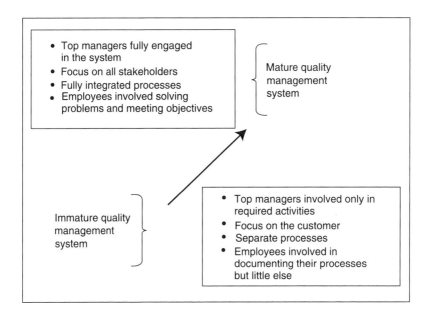

Figure 1.2   Involvement of people in immature and mature quality management systems.

processes of the management system work together to achieve the organization's objectives. Integration also means the people of the organization share a culture committed to continual improvement.

Figure 1.2 provides an example of the maturity concept using the principle "involvement of people."

THE DILEMMA

Quality management systems that focus on such business results as reducing costs may ignore the very focus on stakeholder interests needed to achieve long-term excellence. And yet, failure to perform in the present will deny the organization any future at all.

The dilemma involves objectives that appear to conflict. Of course, mature systems have advantages. But wait a moment; isn't it important to first implement a basic system? Isn't it important to focus on the customer? Isn't meeting customer expectations the most important thing an organization does? Don't regulators expect some sort of independent quality function in some industries? Should we not be doing all the things necessary to meet customer requirements and achieve performance excellence at the same time? It is obvious that we should, but we can't do everything at the same time. Priorities are important, and placing our priorities on meeting customer requirements may well be the first step, but what do we do next?

The Solution

You might consider a quality management system that achieves minimal conformance to ISO 9001:2000 to be somewhat immature. But it would not be correct to assume that a system that uses every one of the ideas suggested in ISO 9004:2000 is very mature. In fact, such a system might very well be an overburdening bureaucracy. Some winners of quality awards have been unable to sustain the levels of excellence that they displayed when they won the award and some organizations have based their very mature systems on ISO 9001 alone. Mature systems are best built by using ISO 9001:2000, ISO 9004:2000, and the excellence criteria such as EFQM or Baldrige together, but the criteria used are far less important than how those criteria are implemented. The solution is to base quality management systems on principles, not just on specific criteria. This means that organizations should develop an understanding of how the principles apply in their own situations. To do this, an organization should use the principles described earlier in this chapter to develop its own internal principles of organizational quality management. These internal principles can then be used to provide a guiding light for implementing, maintaining, and improving the organization's quality management system. *By using principles, we have a means to test each decision we make when faced with the dilemmas posed by conflicting objectives.* This gives the quality management system a broad focus.

The Mature Quality Management System:
- Built on ISO 9001:2000
- Focused on performance improvement
- Based on the principles
- Continually assessed for excellence

THE PRINCIPLES AND ORGANIZATIONAL TRANSFORMATION

Mission, Vision, and Business Model

To many, the subject of organizational mission and vision statements brings back memories of long and tiresome sessions to develop words of little meaning. Such wasteful exercises need to be avoided. These topics are serious, and addressing them is vital to success. *Mission* is the description of why the organization exists, and *vision* describes a picture of where the organization is going to be in the future. These are not trivial, soft topics. Instead they are the essence of understanding an organization. During the time a new business is being developed, these are clear, at least to the person or group of people who started the business. They are based on the start-up management's ideas and personal goals for their venture. In fact, the top leaders of many successful new companies can talk of little else but what their new business is (its mission) and where it is going (its vision). As a few employees are added, deployment of the mission and vision is easy because the top leaders talk about it all the time. In fact, these are often written down as a part of the business plan developed to get financing for the new venture. As time goes on the organization grows. It moves into new markets, hires new people, and may move into larger quarters. Communications become more complex, and the clarity of overall business purpose and direction is often clouded or lost. Top managers may still know it, but they may not talk about it very often.

Maintaining a constant, clear understanding of the organization's mission and vision is an important prerequisite to success because full alignment of the system and its processes with business needs requires an understanding of basic direction.

> Mission: What is our business?
> Vision: What do we want our business to be like in the future?

The basic business model must also be well understood. As changes in the external environment occur, top leaders may need to rethink some of these basic concepts about the business and the impact of change on its mission and vision. This is the "how" associated with the mission. It is the answer to questions like: What is our target market? How do we make money? What is our competitive advantage? How will our resources be provided? How will we ensure sufficient cash flow?

Developing the Organization's Own Organizational Quality Management Principles

Once an organization has a clear understanding of its basic mission and a vision of the future, it can develop an understanding of the guiding principles that will help it accomplish its mission in the near term and lead it toward that vision. At its simplest, this means translating the principles of organizational quality management discussed earlier in this chapter into the language of your own organization and then comparing them to your organization's mission, vision, and business model. This process must involve the top managers of the organization and the ultimate words should be theirs.

The process for developing your own principles starts with an assessment by top management. One approach would be to give each top manager a form similar to Table 1.4. Ask each of them to determine the importance of each organizational quality management principle and relate each principle to the organization's business.

Table 1.4   Organizational analysis against the 12 principles of organizational management.

1 Principle	2 What activities are important related to the principle?	3 How important is each activity? Rank each from 1 = low to 5 = critical	4 How well do we do each activity? Rank each from 1 = poor to 5 = excellent	5 Score: multiply column 3 and column 4 scores.
Customer focus				
Focus on other stakeholders (social responsibility)				
Focus on results				
Focus on agility				
Focus on the future				
Leadership, vision, and purpose				
Establish and align objectives				
Manage a system of interrelated processes				
Manage with facts supported by credible data				
Improve, innovate, and learn				
Develop and involve people				
Develop suppliers, partners, and other stakeholders				

A simple process for this might be:

- Ask the members of top management to make their own assessment and develop his or her own scoring.

- Hold a facilitated meeting and reach consensus on which activities are most important to the organization.

- Consolidate the activities and group them by related principle.

- Draft a set of principles for the organization.

- Conduct multiple reviews by the whole top management group until there is agreement on the organization's principles.

The process is easy to describe, but gaining committed agreement among the key top managers is often difficult and time consuming. During the development process, the top management team should take the time to consider how the organization's principles will be deployed. They should consider the methods to be used for deployment and the timing. If you are not serious about it, don't even start. But if you take the time to do it right, the result will be worth the effort. An agreed-to set of principles can be the bedrock for organizational excellence.

Some organizations have lengthy lists of principles and may include more than those discussed earlier in this chapter or some may be split into multiple items. As an example, some organizations may have principles around both the idea of a "systems approach to management" and the "process approach." This approach has the advantage of stating most or all of what is important to the organization in one place.

Other organizations may have very short lists of principles, expressing the very few basic ideas that are important in each item's title. Other concepts can be combined and built in as part of explanatory text. For example, an organization might have just three principles, but each may cover other critical issues such as:

- **Focus on results**—Explaining that results related to customers and other stakeholders, speed and agility, and sustainability of the enterprise are the results that are important.

- **Leadership**—Explaining that leaders must create an environment and provide resources to involve all employees, that they must manage using facts and data, that they must provide visionary leadership, and that they must develop employees and suppliers to support the organization's success.

- **Continual improvement**—Explaining which focus areas and core competencies are important for improvement, innovation, and organizational learning.

Short lists have one compelling characteristic: they are simple and their titles are easy to remember. The disadvantage of the short list approach is that it is easy for a simple memorized list to send the wrong signals. For example, the principle "focus on results" can, over time, come to mean meeting expected financial results alone.

The length of the organization's list of principles is not important. It is important that each principle be stated in clear, concise language. They must also be explained to everyone in the organization. It is critical that they reflect the real beliefs and intent of the very top managers. They must be useful for testing the organization's behaviors over time.

Using Your Organizational Quality Management Principles in Managing Change

Organizations that are intent on making dramatic improvements in performance will need to plan and make the changes necessary to get those gains. The changes should be guided by the organization's principles. The principles are guideposts that are useful in making decisions and taking action. If an organization has done a sloppy job of understanding its principles, there will be a temptation to change or abandon the principles when the organization faces adversity. If the principles have been well thought out with the organization's mission, vision, and business model in mind, then the principles should form a solid foundation on which adversity can be faced and changes can be made.

Assess the Organization's Use of *Your* Principles

Development of organizational principles started with an assessment against the 12 organizational quality management principles. It is sensible to reassess every year or so how well the organization is doing in its actions and behaviors relative to the organization's own principles. This type of assessment should have at least three components:

- Perceptions of top managers

- Perceptions of other members of the organization using a cross-section of organizational functions and levels

- Perceptions of other key stakeholders

This type of assessment may involve complex surveys, or it may be done over a short period using a few focus groups. The objective is to develop an honest understanding of how well the organization is applying its principles and to develop action plans to improve where necessary. Table 1.5 is an example of a format that can be used to develop this information.

Table 1.5   Form of output of periodic assessment of principle effectiveness.

Principle: _____	
Important activities to do when considering this principle	How well our organization does each activity
What actions will you take?	

It should be remembered that when we measure perception of how well a principle is being applied, we are, in a sense, attempting to measure the culture of the organization. It can be tempting to look at overall attitudes related to a principle rather than at the actual activities that are important in the principle's use. It is useful to resist that temptation. Direct measurement of culture is difficult. Making direct changes to cultures is even harder. Rather, it is easier to measure how well the important activities are being

! carried out. *It is far easier to convince people to change what they do (activities and behaviors) than it is to change attitudes and beliefs.* If an organization insists that the needed activities and behaviors be carried out, and if these activities produce results, attitudes—and over time the culture—will change as well. We will discuss organizational cultures further in Chapter 4.

Assessments of this nature should be infrequent (with three to five years between them) and well planned.

USING THE PRINCIPLES OF ORGANIZATIONAL QUALITY MANAGEMENT

There is no single panacea for organizational performance improvement, much less for organizational excellence. Just using the organizational quality management principles alone is seldom enough because the principles do not get at all the details an organization must manage to be successful. But there is nothing an organization can do that can have more benefit than the development and deployment of its principles. Achieving an understanding of how the principles can be applied can bring new insight. Assessing an organization against these concepts provides the opportunity to use ideas demonstrated to facilitate performance improvement. Organizations should take sufficient the time to develop their own principles. They should understand what activities and behaviors are needed to get the most benefit from each important principle. They should also periodically assess how well they are doing. Organizations can use their own principles to focus energy on improving the behaviors essential to their own future success.

WHAT CAN I DO NOW?

Principles underlie (or should underlie) everything an organization does. Do you know the principles that underlie your quality management system?

Use Table 1.4 as a starting point to develop the principles for your organization. Add, delete, and combine principles listed in the table to arrive at a set of principles that fits the purpose and culture of your organization.

We should caution that formalizing the principles that underlie an organization's quality management system is not a trivial exercise, and it is not one that can be completed by midlevel or frontline managers. Rather, top management participation is required. But it is not necessary to wait for top management! Anyone in the organization can start the process. If the effort has substance, top management has a reasonable probability of becoming engaged.

2

Engage Top Management

A man of words and not of deeds
Is like a garden full of weeds.
And when the weeds begin to grow,
It's like a garden full of snow.

Old English nursery rhyme

Once an organization has a clear definition and understanding of the principles that will guide its policies, procedures, and decision making, it can focus on applying those principles to achieve performance improvement. In the remaining chapters, we will explain approaches organizations can consider for accelerating quality management from minimum compliance with organizational and internationally accepted quality management system standards (for example, ISO 9001:2000) to a higher level of maturity, sophistication, and effectiveness.

In the research conducted while developing the functional requirements specification for ISO 9001:2000, a survey was made of more than 1100 organizations worldwide (43 countries represented). The survey included large and small organizations operating in a diversity of markets (hardware, software, services, and processed materials). A common theme emerging from this survey was that the next generation of ISO 9001 needed to require increased involvement of top management in the quality management process. Interesting!

WHAT MOTIVATES TOP MANAGEMENT

How can a quality management system standard require the involvement of top management?

It is true that words were put into 9001:2000 to "require top management to . . . ." Indeed, every subclause in Clause 5 starts with the words "Top management shall . . . ." But stating such "requirements" in a standard does not mean that top management will be motivated to embrace the activities prescribed by the standard. Yet a quality management system without enthusiastic top management involvement is doomed to failure.

Is this a paradox? It could be, but not necessarily. Let's think about this.

What is the role of top management in any organization? The classic responsibilities of top management have been described by many and in many different ways—and they can be broadly categorized as follows: Top management is responsible for planning, organizing, leading, and controlling an organization to achieve identified results. What results, one might ask? The results that the organization plans to achieve. *If there are no plans, then any results should be satisfactory.*

So top management is or should be motivated and compensated to produce planned results. If the organization is an army, a desired result could be the capture of a hill or a country. If the organization is a manufacturer, planned results could be maintaining a market share 5 percent greater than any competitor, at a profit margin of at least X percent.

To understand how to engage top management, first let's consider what motivates top management.

Quality per se does *not* motivate top managers.

A top manager once made an analogy between his organization and the human body. There needs to be a balance among the various elements of the body. It serves no purpose to have the strongest human heart if the lungs do not function. Likewise, the best technical product in a marketplace is doomed to failure without effective marketing, and the best product with the greatest marketing is doomed without production capability.

So, it is typical that top managers are (or should be) motivated to achieve balance across an organization. They perceive that they need this balance to produce the planned results. They are also motivated to champion activities and projects that contribute to achieving and maintaining this balance. They may not even be conscious of this motivation.

What are some of the key activities that top managers consider to be important? These activities will vary by organization, depending on profit motivation (nonprofit organizations may be different from for-profit organizations), product maturity, competitive environment, and many other factors. In a typical manufacturing-based organization, a listing of key performance indicators could include items such as sales, market share, costs, profit margins, inventory turnover, and percentage of personnel fully qualified. One common approach to articulating key indicators is the Balanced Scorecard approach of categorizing key performance indicators into four key areas:

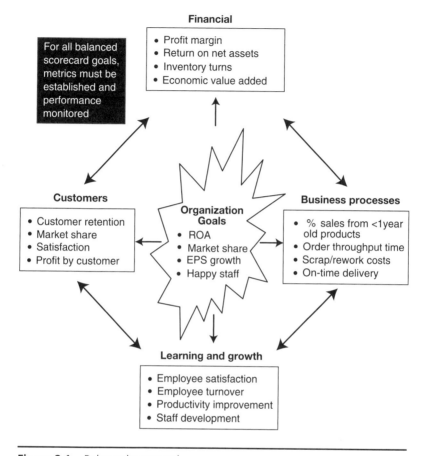

Figure 2.1   Balanced scorecard.

(1) financial, (2) business processes, (3) learning and growth, and (4) customers.[1] This concept is illustrated in Figure 2.1.

In a for-profit organization (especially publicly held organizations), the areas that tend to receive the highest interest and attention are those found on the income statement and the balance sheet. But, income and balance sheet figures are results driven by activities in the organization. Herein is a great opportunity: relating quality to financial results!

To achieve full and active engagement of top management in the quality quest for an organization, the quality proposition must be postured in a way that is viewed as a contributor to achieving organizational goals. This means the quality proposition in for-profit organizations must be shown to improve the income statement and balance sheet items. In not-for-profit organizations, the quality proposition must help achieve defined, stated, and planned results; consistent with the charter and tax status of the organization.

If quality is not positioned as a vital element of accomplishing the objectives of the organization, then there is little hope that full engagement of top management in the quality management system will be achieved.

The need for such thinking is not obvious when reading the ISO 9001:2000 requirements for a minimum quality management system. It does become clearer in the Baldrige and European Foundation for Quality Management (EFQM) criteria.

On this issue, it is fortunate that ISO 9001:2000 provides a starting point for at least opening the conversation with top management. This starting point is the several specific requirements that top managers must accomplish. Dealing with these issues can give top managers better insight into the actions they need to take to achieve financial results through quality improvements.

Consider the following examples of requirements directed at top managers:

5.1   " . . . evidence of commitment . . ."

5.2   ". . . ensure that customer requirements . . ."

5.3   ". . . ensure that the quality policy . . ."

5.4.1 ". . . ensure that quality objectives . . ."

5.4.2 ". . . ensure that . . . planning of the quality management system . . ."

5.5.1 ". . . responsibilities and authorities are defined . . ."

5.5.2 ". . . appoints a member of management . . ."

5.5.3 ". . . appropriate communication . . ."

5.6.1 ". . . review the organization's QMS . . ."

There is an opportunity to demonstrate a "payoff" for top management to address each of these requirements. But such involvement is not automatic and all too often it is nonexistent. Organizational lip service is all too frequently the norm. Instead, quality leaders need to convince top managers to implement processes of substance consistent with organization principles.

Before considering how we can engage top management in addressing these requirements, let's consider a few of the reasons why top management has not been engaged in the quality process.

INTEGRATION OF QUALITY MANAGEMENT WITH THE PURPOSES OF THE ORGANIZATION

In many organizations (perhaps most organizations), the role of quality has not been considered in strategic thinking and planning. CEOs, CFOs, marketing development VPs, and manufacturing VPs sit around a long polished wooden table to plot the destiny of the organization over the next two to five years. It is typical for the role of product or service quality to be ignored when issues such as market share, margin, market expansion, and cash flow are addressed. The consequences of such a strategic planning methodology are that product or service quality is not integral to the activities of the organization. Quality is, at best, a tactic for preventing nonconforming products or services from reaching an end-customer. The quality activities are thus outside the basic decision-making process of the organization. The organization's decision makers do not view them as an integral element of the management of the organization.

If top management is not including consideration of quality-related issues in strategic planning or mainstream organization management, the quality professionals need to try to "force the issue." The concepts discussed later in this chapter and those in other chapters (Chapters 4, 6, and 10 in particular) can be used to enhance the probability of success for integration of quality thinking into the mainstream of the management of an organization.

EMPHASIS ON PROCESS AND PERFORMANCE RATHER THAN PAPER

Another issue existing in many organizations is that quality management has been positioned as a collection of activities driven by procedures, policies, and other forms of documentation. Such systems have the appearance that paper is the goal. ISO 9001:1987 and ISO 9001:1994, for example, helped perpetuate this view by their dominant focus on documented procedures, not customer satisfaction. ISO 9001:2000 has demystified this situation, as there is now a clear focus on results that are valued by customers.

UNDERSTANDING THE ROLE OF QUALITY MANAGEMENT

Very few top executives of organizations have worked as quality professionals. And very few dedicate time or effort to learning the tools of quality.

More likely, top managers have risen to executive positions via sales, marketing, finance, or technology. In many small and medium-size businesses, top managers and business owners are entrepreneurs but not trained business managers. Thus, there is often a profound lack of understanding of the role that quality management could play in a contemporary organization.

QUALITY-SPEAK VS. MONEY-SPEAK

Perhaps the most significant barrier to the detachment exhibited by top managers to quality management is the fact that quality professionals have not been effective in their communications with top managers.

> "We have met the enemy and they are us."
> Pogo

The language of top managers is money. The language of quality is quality-speak. Quality professionals talk about nonconformities, designed experiments, variation, process capability, and many arcane acronyms such as UCL, DOE, and AQL.

Consider a simple test of your money-vs. quality-speak vocabulary. How many of the following 10 terms are recognized and understood?

ISO 9001	AQL
TQM	FMEA
MBNQA	QFD
MTBF	PDCA
UCL	APQP

How many of the following 10 terms are recognized and understood?

RONA	SEC
NPV	IPO
LIBOR	NYSE
EPS	ERISA
FASB	EBITDA

In a normal seminar group, quality professionals can identify eight or more for the first set and three or fewer for the second set. And under similar circumstances, results for executive management are exactly the opposite. Quality professionals have created barriers to engaging top management by not being able to speak the language of top managers. If one is in Italy and wants to eat, one needs to be able to speak at least some Italian to communicate at all. If one is trying *to engage top managers* in quality management, *the quality professional needs to be able to speak the language of management—money.*

For the meanings of the acronyms, see Table 2.1.

Table 2.1   Quality-speak differs from management-speak.

Quality-speak		Management-speak	
ISO 9001	ISO 9001:2000 Quality management system Requirements	RONA	Return on net assets
		NPV	Net present value
MBNQA	Malcolm Baldrige National Quality Award	LIBOR	London Inter-Bank Offered Rate
MTBF	Mean time between failures	EPS	Earnings per share
UCL	Upper control limit	FASB	Financial Accounting Standards Board
AQL	Acceptance quality limit	SEC	Securities and Exchange Commission
FMEA	Failure modes and effects analysis		
QFD	Quality function deployment	IPO	Initial public offering
PDCA	Plan, Do, Check, Act (the Deming/Shewart cycle)	NYSE	New York Stock Exchange
		ERISA	Employee Retirement Income Security Act
APQP	Advanced product quality planning	EBITDA	Earnings before interest, taxes, depreciation, and amortization
TQM	Total quality management		

HOW TO ENGAGE TOP MANAGERS

We all know that there is no magic potion to infuse into the organization's water supply that will create an environment in which top management embraces quality management. Rather, it is the *responsibility* of the quality professionals to learn how to communicate with top management in such a way that the business managers *want* to be fully engaged in the quality process.

Techniques to Encourage Full Engagement of Top Management

We suggest the practice of eight virtues by quality professionals to enhance the engagement of top management in the quality process. These virtues are:

1. Talk with top managers in their language.

2. Incorporate quality management into strategic and tactical planning.

3. Embrace customer sastisfaction throughout the organization.

4. Embrace continual improvement throughout the organization.

5. Take the objectives process seriously.

6. Ensure that quality performance indicators are integral to performance reviews.

7. Gather, analyze, and act on quality cost data.

8. Make the management review process into an activity that top management values.

These eight virtues are not the only virtues for quality professionals to practice, but they are a good starting point. Before we complain "that top management is not fully engaged in the quality process of the organization," we should ask ourselves if we are doing our part all of the time, every day of the year, to motivate top managers.

Let's look at each of these virtues in detail and consider activities and behaviors that will improve the engagement of top management.

The Language of Managers

Earlier we indicated that a major barrier to top managers' full engagement in the quality process is that the quality value proposition is often presented in quality-speak, such as defects, complaints, rejects, and control limits. To engage and create top management interest, it is far more effective to take the next step and convert the quality-speak into money-speak. For example, 24 customer complaints last month could be conveyed as, "Last month we experienced 24 complaints for our Flimflam product line; the total cost of resolving each complaint was $1000 as measured by Accounting, resulting in a bottom line negative impact of $24,000, which annualized could be a drain of $288,000. At our net profit of 10%, we would have to generate close to $3,000,000 in sales to offset the cost of tolerating this level of complaints. And, as Dr. W. Edwards Deming was fond of saying, the cost of damage to our reputation is 'unknown and unknowable.' "[2] Such a positioning should get the attention and engagement of top managers, perhaps even to a level beyond that desired by some members of the organization. But it is normal for such engagement to elicit the commitment of resources needed to address the causes of the customer complaints.

So, the *virtue* to be practiced is to *talk with top managers in their language.*

Quality in the Planning Process

To be considered serious contributors to organizational success, quality professionals are encouraged to demonstrate why and how quality needs to be an element of strategic and tactical planning. Like we described earlier, all elements of the organization need to work in balance, with quality being an important dimension.

It is not enough to pronounce that top management should consider quality in strategic planning. Rather, the criticality of considering the quality dimension needs to be amply demonstrated in order to attract the attention of top management. For example, let's consider new-product planning. Quality could show, via analysis of customer satisfaction data, those features and benefits of high interest to potential customers. Or in projecting the cost of goods sold (CGS, another of the terms top managers revere), the quality professional could contribute trend analysis of process performance to model costs with anticipated improvements over the planning horizon, thereby influencing pricing strategy.

To get top managers to include quality inputs to planning, the quality professional needs to present the value of his or her participation in terms of achieving organizational objectives. He or she should not advocate quality for the sake of quality alone.

The *virtue* to be practiced is to *align quality planning with principles* and *incorporate quality planning into the strategic and tactical business planning of the organization.*

Customer Satisfaction

Data abound to demonstrate that there is substantial ROI (return on investment—another of those top management terms) related to investing in the retention of existing customers. Conversely, the cost and potential damage to the organization caused by a dissatisfied customer is high. Research indicates that one dissatisfied customer will bad-mouth the offending organization (guilty or not) to at least 10 potential customers if their complaint or dissatisfaction is not resolved.[3]

Data also exist to demonstrate that it is at least five times more expensive to find a new customer than to keep an existing customer.[4]

Data thus support the intuitively obvious fact that customers are important to an organization.

The importance of customer satisfaction needs to be in the forefront of top management communications. We need to quantify the leverage customer satisfaction brings to increased sales revenues and profit margins. We need to quantify the cost or negative impact of not satisfying customers. Such quantification often demonstrates that customer dissatisfaction can have its root cause in any area of the organization. For example, the sales people may have overpromised, the design may not be robust, the production process may have introduced flaws in manufacturing, poorly trained service delivery staff may have angered the customer, support services may have provided poor product documentation, or there may be invoicing issues in finance.

Exposing the sources and implications of customer dissatisfaction communicates the message that the entire organization owns customer satisfaction. And this communication can make it clear that the entire organization needs to be engaged in ensuring that we meet our commitments to customers. When this message has been made clear, it is a good time to get key parts of the organization to establish and measure performance against objectives that are tied to customer satisfaction.

The *virtue* to be practiced is to *embrace customer satisfaction throughout the organization* to the extent that every individual understands his or her responsibility for contributing to the organization's specific objectives that are focused on customers.

Continual Improvement

An organization is like a living organism; it is either growing or dying, either getting better or getting worse. Most top managers are easy to engage if we identify opportunities for improvement, propose objectives that will generate results, and offer improvement tools that have a history of achieving the promised gains.

Continual Improvement requires the commitment and involvement of top managers, but it also relies on hard work. The strategies given in the other chapters of this book can help in carrying out that hard work. Perhaps most important to achieving a culture in which improvement becomes a continual reality are the alignment and process management strategies discussed in Chapters 4 and 5. Chapter 6 discusses the actions that can be taken to fully embrace continual improvement.

The *virtue* to be practiced is to *embrace continual improvement throughout the organization* to the extent that every individual understands his or her responsibility for identifying and meeting improvement objectives.

Quality Objectives

There is a requirement in ISO 9001:2000 that quality objectives be established at "relevant functions and levels" in an organization. This requirement presents an opportunity to ensure that top management aligns the quality policy with the organization's mission, vision, and business objectives. Then objectives can be developed by top management for the organization. This may be a cascade process, with all top managers assuming at least one objective related to fulfillment of the pronouncements in the quality policy and then ensuring that their direct reports have objectives similarly aligned. This can be done in a minimalist manner, to show some evidence of addressing the ISO 9001 requirement or it can be done in a way that engages the entire organization in achieving organizational objectives, goals defined in business plans, and the statements made in the quality policy. In many organizations, some portion of executive compensation is tied to the achievement of objectives, including quality objectives. The quality professional needs to be prepared to show top managers how they can be engaged in meeting the ISO 9001 requirement for quality objectives in a way that goes beyond lip service. Chapter 4 discusses aligning quality objectives and business objectives.

The *virtue* to be practiced is to *take the objectives process seriously* as an activity important to the organization's performance and survival.

Reviewing Organization Results

Organizations need to have regular reviews of organizational performance. There are many tactics that are used for these reviews. Some organizations do very formal reviews, while other organizations have very informal ways to review progress. Some perform reviews on an ad hoc basis while others do them at specific intervals, such as weekly, monthly, or quarterly. Some have a loose agenda, some no agenda at all, and some a well structured agenda. Some use Balanced Scorecards, some chart rooms, some circulate reams of performance data beforehand for discussion during operations review meetings.

No matter what the form or formality of such operational reviews, the quality professional should be able to make a compelling case to top management to include in such reviews key performance indicators relating to process performance and product conformity. If key indicators of high interest to the quality professional do not have equal visibility with other operating indicators (such as sales, shipments, or costs), then top management will not be engaged in any initiatives relating to such indicators. The essential issue is for the quality professional to justify the inclusion of quality indicators, to create the environment where top management wants to and insists on seeing performance results in the key quality areas. This justification becomes easy when the quality objectives are linked to the overall business objectives of the organization. We will explore this alignment in more detail in Chapter 4.

The *virtue* to be practiced is to *ensure that quality performance indicators are an integral element* of the performance review.

Understanding Quality Costs

The concept of gathering costs related to quality (and unquality) has been in the literature since at least the early 1950s. Joe Juran's first *Quality Control Handbook* had a chapter on "The Economics of Quality," and Val Feigenbaum dedicated a chapter of his 1961 classic *Total Quality Control* to Quality Costs. Quality Costs are discussed in Chapter 5 in both books (both are worth reading), and both propose models that include Prevention, Appraisal, Internal Failure, and External Failure categories for quantifying quality costs. And one of the most popular books published by Quality Press is *Principles of Quality Costs*[5] (a product of the ASQ Quality Costs Committee), which proposes a similar basic model.

Even though this methodology has been around for quite a while and has been embraced by leading quality thinkers, its acceptance and systematic use has not been universal. This is particularly true for smaller organizations. Perhaps the rigor of creating the model and establishing the accounting mechanisms to gather such data are viewed as too onerous. Perhaps the "fear of the unknown world of accounting" causes quality professionals to avoid this methodology, while at the same time they become enthusiastic about diving into Six Sigma initiatives even without knowing what a random variable is or why moment generating functions are important.

We believe that if it is desired to engage top management in the quality process, a virtue well worth cultivating is the understanding and promotion of Quality Costs concepts, no matter how big or small the organization. The references indicated above, and many others, describe how to approach this subject. Our purpose here is to encourage use of the concept because it is one of the most effective tools available to engage top management in the quality process. Why? It describes issues in a language that management understands—money. And if the finance department participates in the creation of the databases and reports, then the reports become even more compelling to top management. Talking money ensures engagement.

The *virtue* to be practiced is to *gather, analyze, and act on quality cost data.*

Management Review

A management review process is required by ISO 9001:2000. So for the quality professional desiring to fully engage top management, this requirement presents a real opportunity. The challenge is to ensure that the management review process is viewed as a positive force in driving organizational improvement, not just another meeting.

The quality professional can employ many techniques to ensure that management review is effective and embraced by top management. These techniques include:

- Keeping the meetings short (2 hours or less is recommended)

- Ensuring agendas and reference materials are distributed well before the meetings

- Insisting that inputs to management review encourage management decision making (not just data but rather analyzed data)

- Including issues that are forward looking

- Keeping the meeting focused

- Maintaining a focus on issues that have the greatest impact on customer satisfaction

- Ensuring great minutes are promptly distributed with clear action items and responsibilities

Even though top management should run the management review meetings, the quality professionals need to operate behind the scenes, ensuring that they are viewed as a productive use of top management time.

The *virtue* to be practiced is to *make the management review process into an activity that top management values,* not just endures.

ENGAGING TOP MANAGERS

The complaint that it is difficult or impossible to engage top management in the quality process is one of the most common themes voiced by quality professionals. The major issue is often not with top management. Rather, it is with the processes employed to engage the top managers. If a combination of the approaches described in this chapter is employed, we believe that top managers will become more engaged and will want—even demand—greater involvement in decision making to drive improvements, perhaps even more so than desired by the quality professionals.

WHAT CAN I DO NOW?

Think about the eight virtues that can be practiced to enhance the engagement of top management in the quality process. How does your organization rate for the practice of these virtues across the organization?

Perform a mini self-assessment to evaluate the degree to which each of the virtues is an ingrained "way of life." If a virtue is not embraced throughout the organization, what could or should be done, if anything, to encourage the practice of that virtue?

3

Shift the Focus from Internal Operations to the External Customer

"Hell is the place where the satisfied compare disappointments."

Philip Moeller
Madame Sand

Why are customers important? Only because without customers an organization has no reason to exist.

Customers provide the cash that enables the organization to continue to exist.

Even in the not-for-profit world or in government organizations, customers are important, even though there may be no direct profit motive associated with the products or services provided. If there were no customers, there would be no need for the organization. There is also the privatization concept. The threat of privatization should motivate government organizations everywhere to consider the intensity of focus on the end customer. Ultimately, taxpayers are the customers who are funding the government activity, and taxpayers are intent on securing fair value for taxes paid.

We should remind the reader that in this chapter, and indeed throughout this book, when we are talking about customers we are referring to external customers. Not that internal customers are not important; they are. External customers, however, are vital. This chapter provides insight into approaches that an organization can use to understand and satisfy those external customers.

INTERNAL FOCUS

Many years ago, an individual walking in the center of a city came upon a construction site. Being curious, the individual asked a worker, "What are you doing?" The worker replied, "I am laying stones. All day long I lay stones." Walking a little further, there was another person performing what appeared to be the same kind of work. So the question was asked again, "What are you doing?" The answer was a little surprising: "I am participating in the building of a cathedral. People will come from far and wide to worship in this beautiful place."

Same jobs—very different perspectives of the responsibilities of the individuals involved and their perceptions of the objectives of the work being performed!

Does this perspective influence how the job is performed? Very likely.

In many organizations, managers do not promote focus on the end customer as a prime expectation of everyone in the organization. Rather, like the first bricklayer, jobs are often viewed as moving pallets from station to station, putting clean towels in the hotel rooms, or writing software code. Objectives for such jobs might be moving 100 pallets per hour, or putting clean towels in 27 rooms per day, or writing 200 lines of code per day. Although the specific requirements and measures for each activity may be clear, the underlying reason for doing the activity—to ensure the satisfaction of the end-customer—has not been communicated throughout the organization,

The concepts related to quality have progressed in recent years from quality control to quality assurance to quality management to total quality management. This shift has brought increasing attention to control of processes instead of inspecting individual items. But even today in many organizations, delivering a product or service to a customer is organized and performed as a series of discrete, sometimes disconnected processes. In Chapter 5 we will discuss processes in greater detail and describe how process management is critical to focusing the energies and talent of an organization.

Although it may be subtle, and even though they often voice the comment that "our organization is concerned with satisfying customers," most organizations do not universally focus on the customer. In a typical organization it is rare for everyone to feel true ownership of end-customer satisfaction. This is often true, even though the principles and objectives of the organization may state that satisfying external customers is the primary focus of the organization. Why this internal focus? Top managers may not intend the organization to be so focused on internal activities, and top managers often express frustration that the organization places too little importance on the customer. More often than not, the internal focus exists because the actions of the organization's quality leaders and top managers do not send signals that customers are important. There may be a lot of talk about customer focus, but leaders must make that talk real through actions.

There is much in the literature to support this notion that it is imperative to focus the organization on satisfying customers. As was mentioned in Chapter 2, one generalization is that a dissatisfied customer tells 10 people he or she is not satisfied.[1] In addition, there is much research to indicate that dissatisfied customers do not complain; rather, depending on the severity of the complaint and economic loss, they just defect!

Other research compares the cost of finding a new customer vs. retaining an existing customer. Without delving into the details that were discussed in Chapter 2, it requires many times more investment to find a new customer than to retain an existing customer. Indeed, preserving the current customer base is one of the cornerstone strategies of organizations that desire to obtain and sustain double-digit growth rates.[2]

So from several viewpoints, *a core value of the organization needs to be to focus on the end-customer.* If resources are limited (and they always are), this means that our priorities need to be those actions, projects, and organizational initiatives that will strengthen "customer first" values. We need performance measures that drive behaviors aligned with these values. This philosophy should be in direct alignment with the organization's principles we discussed in Chapter 1. Achieving this alignment is discussed in Chapter 4.

USING QUALITY MANAGEMENT TO FOCUS THE ENTIRE ORGANIZATION ON THE CUSTOMER

The ISO 9001:2000 model is well known by now. Its simplest form is illustrated in Figure 3.1.

The customer speaks, and the organization listens and delivers what the customer wants, needs, desires, or at the very least, has stated as requirements. The organization should analyze customer data to determine what outcomes are wanted by customers. Then actions need to be focused on ensuring that the organization's products and services provide the needed outcomes.

If we accept the premise that customers (except those not worth keeping) are of paramount importance, how can an organization use the Quality Management System to enhance its focus on external customers?

The ISO 9001:2000 model encourages an organization to focus on its end-customers in several ways. How an organization addresses customer

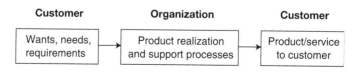

Figure 3.1 The basic process model.

focus, and how the leaders mold the organization's behavior in this area, can profoundly affect the perception of the value of the goods or services it provides. The spectrum of possibilities ranges from a casual or cursory focus on the customer to true belief that customers are of paramount importance. When that belief exists, top managers tend to encourage everyone in the organization to do their jobs in a way that contributes to achieving customer satisfaction. In the more enlightened organizations, the culture is one of striving to obtain customer loyalty by ensuring that every "customer touch point" is a positive experience.

Let's consider a few of the aspects of quality management and how they can be addressed to ensure a sharp focus on end-customers:

- Customer requirements

- Process approach

- Policy, objectives, and alignment

- Management review

- Internal audit

- Customer satisfaction

CUSTOMER REQUIREMENTS

Often meeting customer desires is complicated because customers do not tell us all of their requirements. In fact, *for most products and services it is normal to have a mixture of stated and unstated customer requirements.*

Stated requirements are the things the customer tells us when making the commitment to buy from us. For example, when booking a hotel room, the customer may specify that a king-size bed is required and that the room must be a no-smoking room.

The customer may not have specified that a high-speed Internet connection is needed to connect with her company's network. Having assumed that this will be available, the customer may be very disappointed upon arrival when she discovers that there is no high-speed connection and that the only place to plug in a computer to a dial-in phone line connection is in the hotel lobby! Often organizations must determine unspecified customer needs through surveys, discussions with customers, and customer feedback such as complaints. It is important to address generic expectations specific to the product, service, or sector.

Customers often need or want outcomes more than they want a specific product. In our hotel example, the hotel was ready to provide the outcome of a good night's sleep when what the customer really wanted was to work late into the night on a computer connected to her office network.

For another example, think about the story of a young man who goes to the hospital to be cured of appendicitis. The cure alone is his desired outcome. On the other hand, a cure might not be the best outcome. Perhaps the best possible outcome might be that his appendix is removed, he is cured in a few days, and while in the hospital meets a lovely, very rich young lady on the staff. Later they fall in love and get married. Contrast this with the poor outcome in which the young man is cured of appendicitis, but while in the hospital, he contracts a blood disease and ultimately dies from it. Now, the hospital cannot guarantee every young man a rich wife with each stay! The hospital can identify the possible poor outcomes and work to eliminate their potential causes.

The presence of the telephone data port connection in the hotel room and sanitary conditions to prevent transmission of blood diseases in the hospital are product characteristics that were never specified by the customers in our examples but were needed anyway.

PROCESS APPROACH

The 1987 and 1994 versions of ISO 9001 set a tone for quality management that focused on 20 discrete elements and documented procedures. One could imagine a quality management system developed with 20 isolated elements (silos), with a procedure describing what to do in each silo. This is illustrated in Figure 3.2.

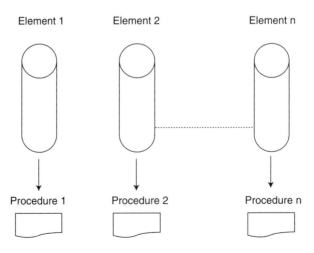

Figure 3.2 The procedure approach to quality management.

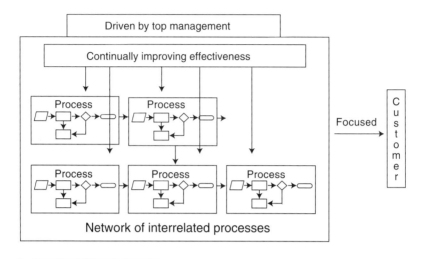

Figure 3.3   The QMS, a network of well-managed processes focused on the customer.

When an organization embraces the process approach (more on this in Chapter 5), the focus of each and every element of the organization is on the requirements (wants, needs, desires) of the end-customer and on internal customers. As illustrated in Figure 3.3, the entire system is focused on meeting customer requirements.

The most important aspects of every job and of all work in the organization are related to knowing that internal customer and external customer requirements are being satisfied. This means that for every process in the organization we need to know the requirements of internal and external customers. We need controls in place to monitor and measure process performance. And we need to monitor and measure product and service conformance so that we know we are meeting requirements. We also should have the records to demonstrate that our processes are running in a way that will result in satisfied customers.

Having and following procedures is important, but every individual in the organization needs to understand that customer satisfaction is paramount. Remember the difference between laying brick and building a cathedral.

POLICY, OBJECTIVES, AND ALIGNMENT

When an organization is serious in its belief that the customer is king or queen, it will ensure that this emphasis is stated in the quality policy and that objectives related to the importance of customers are defined and deployed throughout the organization.

Examples of customer-sensitive objectives could be:

- **CEO**—Visit one customer/month to determine satisfaction with organization performance. Manage the organization in a way that will facilitate a 27 percent improvement in customer satisfaction over two years. The measure of improvement will be the overall score on our annual customer satisfaction survey.

- **COO**—Assume the role of project champion for an improvement project identified from analysis of customer satisfaction data. The objective will be a reduction of customer complaints for the identified issue of at least 20 percent starting three months after project completion.

- **VP of product development**—Use failure modes and effects analysis (FMEA) to identify preventive actions on new product projects. The objective will be a 75 percent reduction in field product reliability problems over a three-year period.

Once an organization begins to think about what everyone can do to enhance customer satisfaction, there will be a free flow of ideas. These ideas will provide more than enough potential objectives. Everyone in the organization can and should have objectives related to the customer. And, in many enlightened organizations, base pay and bonuses are tied, at least in part, to meeting such objectives.

MANAGEMENT REVIEW

Management review is one of the most powerful quality management system activities for ensuring that everyone and everything in the organization is focused on the satisfaction of the end-customer and on creating or expanding customer loyalty.

Management review should not be focused on consideration of day-to-day activities. Rather, it should focus on information related to more global issues such as:

- Results of audits

- Customer feedback

- Process performance and product conformity

- Status of preventive and corrective actions

- Follow-up actions from previous management reviews

- Changes that could affect the quality management system

- Recommendations for improvement

- Planning for resource needs

- Structure, products, and processes of the organization

- Evaluation of supply chain performance

- Development of staff to ensure competence tomorrow

Top management review of these issues presents an opportunity to identify related internal and customer issues. For example, internal product defect data may indicate problems similar to those expressed in customer complaints. Such observations may enable *top managers to identify projects that both improve customer satisfaction and reduce internal costs—at the same time.* Such situations are ideal for emphasizing the paramount importance of directing the attention of the organization to the satisfaction of the end-customer.

INTERNAL AUDIT

Organizations should assess processes in terms of their contribution to customer satisfaction. This means that the emphasis of internal quality audits is directed at ensuring processes and people are functioning to achieve results valued by the end-customer. This cannot be done until auditors are trained and experienced enough to appreciate the outcomes expected by customers and how the organization can ensure those outcomes take place. Figure 3.4 illustrates that procedures and meeting explicit process performance requirements are important, but they are not as important as ensuring that the end-customer will be fully satisfied. Organizations need customers who are eager to speak positively about the goods and services they receive.

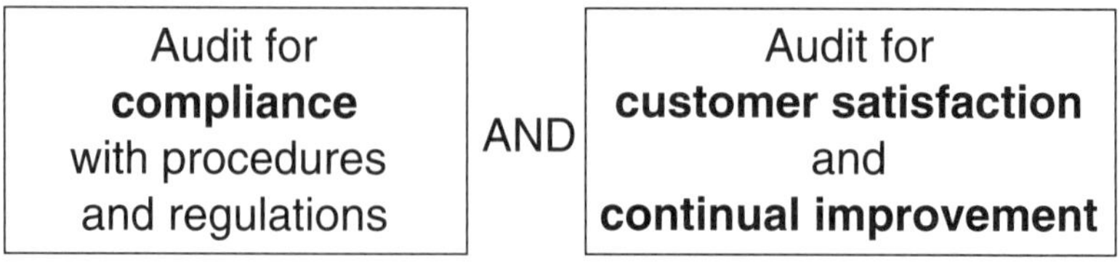

Audit for **compliance** with procedures and regulations	AND	Audit for **customer satisfaction** and **continual improvement**

Figure 3.4   Audits for compliance or for customer satisfaction and continual improvement.

How the internal audit process is structured and implemented, and how internal auditors are trained, will dictate whether an organization has a compliance-oriented internal audit process or a customer satisfaction and continual improvement-oriented audit process. The authors believe in and encourage the latter approach. In Chapter 8 we will discuss in more detail the role of internal quality auditing in the overall management of an organization.

CUSTOMER SATISFACTION

Any organization that has sensitivity to customer satisfaction needs to go far beyond the basic ISO 9001:2000 requirements to be successful.

Customer satisfaction is all about perception. 'Think about staying in a hotel. You, the customer, see little of what actually goes on in running the hotel. You know only what you experienced during your stay. When you check out at 6 A.M., you simply record on the customer comment card that the desk clerk was not very polite when you checked out and complain that there was no hot water this morning. Your perception: "It's a lousy hotel; I won't stay at this one again." In fact you might vow to never use the whole hotel chain again. You will never know that within minutes, maintenance fixed the hot-water problem and the desk clerk no longer had to deal with early risers' calls complaining about it. Almost everyone checking out that morning rates the hotel "one of the best I have stayed in." You will go home and tell 10 of your friends how bad the place was. All the others will quickly forget they had a good experience and tell nobody about it.

You will also never know that the problem with the hot water was caused by the failure of a $1 seal in a newly installed hot water circulating pump. The maintenance manager will return the pump to the plumbing supply company and tell them he wants a different brand—a better pump. The maintenance manager will never know that the pump manufacturer received only a handful of seals from a supplier that were slightly undersize and that only a couple of them actually ended up in completed pumps. Most of the incorrect seals had been found and discarded by the pump manufacturer's assembly team. They only missed a couple. The pump manufacturer's measure of quality for the seals is very high, but our maintenance manager's *perception* is "It's a lousy pump company; I won't buy any more of their pumps." And our maintenance manager will tell about 10 of his friends who also buy pumps about his bad experience.

So sales are gained or lost by customers' perceptions.[3]

Although customer satisfaction has a powerful leverage on profits, many organizations do not have a formalized system for collecting and using customer information. Customer information can relate not only to how customers perceive products and services but also to learning what customers want. If the organization does not know what is important to customers, consistent achievement of customer satisfaction is an impossible dream. All too often the processes to collect and analyze customer information are rudimentary, ad hoc, undocumented, uncontrolled, and underused.

In contrast, the same organization that has a rudimentary system for handling customer data may have a very sophisticated system for handling financial data. Usually there is an entire finance department; a required set of monthly, quarterly, and annual financial reports; a structured review process; a set of decision-making criteria focused on financial measures; and an entire "language" to understand and use financial data.

Modern organizations need good systems for financial and other internal data but, to be competitive, they also need good systems for customer data.

We suggest that top managers can, and should, pay greater attention to obtaining and using customer data, because customer data have a significant potential impact on both long and near-term revenues and margins. Such data can help the organization make changes focused on the future, whereas financial reporting data describe where the organization has been.

One simple approach to learning about the perceptions of our customers is illustrated in Figure 3.5. It is to ask customers for their comments regarding the degree to which a product meets their needs. For example, "On a 10-point scale, with 10 being completely satisfied and 1 being very dissatisfied, how satisfied are you with the service you received on your vehicle during your visit to our dealership service center?"

Questions like this can be asked in telephone interviews, face-to-face discussions, paper surveys, and customer feedback cards.

For organizations that desire to intensify the focus on understanding external customers, ISO 9004:2000 provides guidance that can contribute to

"To what degree are you satisfied with our service center?"

The direct customer interview by telephone is a common tool for monitoring customer perceptions.

Figure 3.5 The telephone is a common tool for talking to customers.

bringing your organization to a reasonable level of customer understanding. ISO 9004 suggests, for example, that an organization establish a process to continually "collect, analyze, and use . . . many sources of customer-related information." Collection can be "active," as when the organization solicits information through surveys, focus groups, and interviews, or it can be "passive," as when customers volunteer complaints, suggestions, and advice.

ISO 9004 goes further than 9001, suggesting that organizations learn "to anticipate future needs." Customer research is a powerful tool for identifying industry trends as well as the specific directions individual customers are pursuing. However, in the thirst for customer data, don't let valuable internal knowledge go untapped. In his lectures, Dr. Deming reminded us, "Did the customer ask for a lightbulb? No. Did the customer ask for the pneumatic tire? No." These innovations came from suppliers who understood customer needs (Deming called this having profound knowledge)—suppliers who knew far better than customers the nature of a specific problem, the capacity of a technology, and the power of a good idea.

The ultimate success of new product ideas that originate within the organization often depends on customer research. Many companies have a "pipeline" of new product ideas or new technologies. Customer research can be used both to prioritize the commercialization of these products and to fine-tune their actual development in order to maximize their desirability in the marketplace.

ISO 9004 also makes the point that organizations should "define . . . the frequency of data-analysis reviews." As was mentioned earlier, most organizations have elaborate systems for the collection, analysis, and review of financial data but have little in place to review customer data. A robust customer satisfaction measurement system could describe when, where, and how customer data should be reviewed.

Customer Satisfaction Measurement—An Example

A common approach to defining, implementing, and documenting a customer satisfaction measurement system could be described as a voice of the customer measurement system. Adoption of this type of process would go beyond the requirements of ISO 9001:2000. But it would also have the more important result of providing meaningful information with which to make strategic and tactical business decisions.

A basic model can be structured in the following four steps: plan your customer data system, gather customer data, understand the data, and deploy the data. These steps can be shown as a cycle, similar to the Shewhart or Deming PDCA cycle (Plan, Do, Check, Act) for quality improvement or in a flowchart. The cycle is illustrated in Figure 3.6.[4]

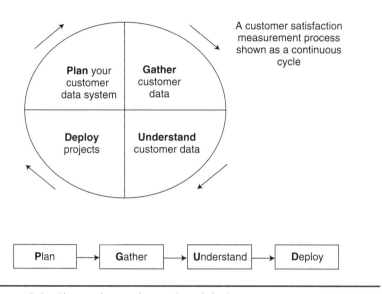

Figure 3.6   Plan, gather, understand, and deploy.
Source: *The ASQ ISO 9000:2000 Handbook*, Figure 29.5.

We have often observed that organizations lack a basic, proactive plan for collecting and using customer data. They react to specific events rather than take the time to develop a comprehensive approach. Often the customer satisfaction measurement process is implemented piecemeal, as if on a "random walk." In one organization, the marketing group had an aggressive customer focus and had developed 43 different methods to gather customer data. Each method grew from some well-intentioned effort, but there was little overall coordination among them, they generated substantial costs, and the use of the data was questionable.

Often organizations do not even have a comprehensive list of the data sources they use or have available. It is not unusual for part of an organization to use one customer data source, while another is unaware of that source and is using something else, perhaps even generating different priorities. Multiple sources of customer data can look like the jumbled puzzle shown in Figure 3.7. This can cause all sorts of expensive problems.

To remedy this situation, it may be worthwhile to establish a process to categorize and inventory the various data collection methods. Such an approach could begin by establishing three primary categories for customer satisfaction data. ISO 9004 suggests two categories of customer data, active and passive. A company collects *active* data by going to the customer and asking deliberate questions or making direct observations of customer behavior. The authors prefer to further split the *passive* into receptive and indirect. *Receptive* data are provided by the customer in the form of complaints or returns. *Indirect* data involves use of secondary sources such as information published in *Quality Digest, Quality Progress,* or in other trade journals. Figure 3.8 shows the relationship among these types of data.

Figure 3.7   Multiple sources of customer data, but unorganized.

Source: *The ASQ ISO 9000:2000 Handbook,* Figure 29.6.

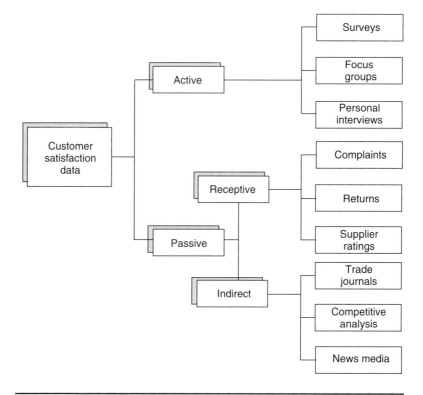

Figure 3.8   Multiple sources of customer data shown in a tree diagram, categorized by data type.

Source: *The ASQ ISO 9000:2000 Handbook,* Figure 29.7.

Knowing and optimizing various sources of customer data may still not be enough. For example, suppose an organization selects four data sources for measuring customer satisfaction. The four data sources are independent, each with its own plan, its own method of gathering data, its own tools for analysis, and even its own approach for deployment. Even though the company is using multiple sources of customer data, the separate analysis results in a significant degradation in value. In this example, the surveys might be analyzed by the marketing department, the focus groups studied by the sales department, the complaints analyzed by customer service, and the media handled by public relations. People are looking at the parts, but who sees the entire picture? This independent data source and analysis situation is illustrated in Figure 3.9.

Many readers probably have systems similar to the one above—your company may be doing something, but it may not be well defined, it may not be documented, and the elements may not be coordinated. A better approach, as shown in Figure 3.10, is to *coordinate during the planning phase, analyze the data from all sources simultaneously, and then have a single unified deployment plan.*

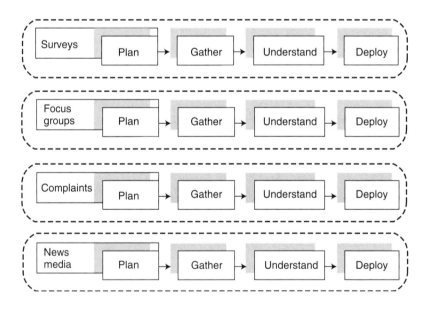

Figure 3.9   Each source of customer data is analyzed and deployed separately, which often leads to confusion and misuse of data.

Source: *The ASQ ISO 9000:2000 Handbook,* Figure 29.8.

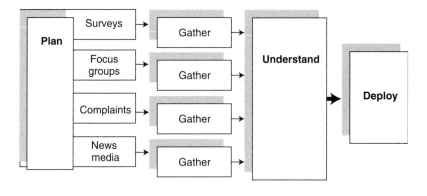

Figure 3.10   A voice of the customer measurement system with four sources of data, a unified planning, holistic analysis, and coordinated action.

Source: *The ASQ ISO 9000:2000 Handbook*, Figure 29.9.

Organizations that believe customers are important will consider such processes, and others, to better understand how to keep existing customers and to attract new customers.

Qualitative vs. Quantitative Customer Information

Another aspect of focusing on the customer is being sensitive to the different kinds of information that can be obtained. Often, if customer information is obtained, it is quantitative; for example, "Tell us your degree of satisfaction with this product on a scale of from 1 to 10" or "Would you buy this product again, yes or no?" Qualitative information, information communicated in words, is often overlooked. Figure 3.11 compares quantitative and qualitative customer information.

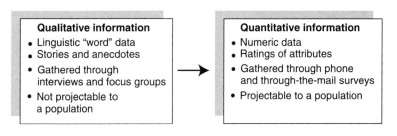

Figure 3.11   Qualitative and quantitative customer information.

Source: *The ASQ ISO 9000:2000 Handbook*, Figure 29.14.

What the customer said	What the customer meant	How important this is	Action	Responsible party
I like the features of . . .				
Your billing department . . .				
I have not heard from your salesman . . .				
Your shipment arrived late again . . .				

Figure 3.12 Pay attention to the customer.

Although *word* data may be more difficult to analyze, it can be a bountiful source of customer information. Modern database management software makes it easy to tabulate and sort such information. A variation of the simple table described in Figure 3.12 could be used to categorize such data and to assist in making decisions (perhaps in management review) on projects to improve performance.

There appears to be broad acceptance of the concept that organizations must be attentive to the needs and requirements of customers to survive and prosper. Every model for quality management (ISO 9001, Baldrige, and European Foundation for Quality Management) emphasizes understanding and satisfying customers. Sector-specific quality models in the telecommunications, aerospace, and automotive industries also emphasize the importance of focusing on knowing and meeting customer requirements.

Emerging thinking such as that found in JIS TRQ0005, discussed in Chapter 1, stresses the importance of *widening satisfied customers* and states that creating customer value is its first principle.

With such potential opportunities to retain existing customers, attract new customers, and improve performance, it is hard to imagine how an organization can work too hard on this issue. It may be the most important issue for the organizational survival.

WHAT CAN I DO NOW?

How many sources of customer information (voices of the customer) exist in your organization? Organizations often have more than 30 sources of customer information about both product and people performance. The sources include customer complaints (via e-mail, formal complaint, phone calls to sales, engineering), surveys conducted by marketing, input from trade shows and on and on.

Sit five people around a table from different areas of an organization and give them each a pad of paper. Ask each person to list all of the organization's sources of customer information. After they have done so, ask them to consolidate their lists. Within 15 minutes most groups identify more than 30 sources of customer information that exist somewhere in the organization.

Does your organization have an approach to using such information to improve product or people performance? Is the information collected and analyzed in any systematic way? Should it be?

What can you conclude about the degree to which your organization is focused on the wants, needs, and requirements of external customers?

4

Achieve Alignment

"Nothing great was ever achieved without enthusiasm"

Ralph Waldo Emerson

From top managers to the lowest level in the organization, from the highest level performance objectives to the targets set for individual processes, alignment is critical. An organization's ability to meet its business performance goals depends on all employees working together with their eyes fixed on common objectives. This chapter discusses the concept of alignment. It reviews alignment of objectives across the organization, alignment of individual objectives with those of the organization, and alignment of the members of the organization in terms of values and attitude.

WHY IS ALIGNMENT SO CRITICAL?

Some might argue that the topic of alignment is a "no-brainer." It may seem obvious that we should align organizational objectives and the actions of all the people in the organization. Yet the authors often see organizations in which the objectives are not even clear, much less aligned. There are many reasons why this is so. In some cases, the organization may never have given thought to its objectives in sufficient detail to commit them to measurable statements. In other cases, top managers may feel constrained and not willing or able to share information about overall business objectives. If your organization has either of these situations, they need to be addressed by the top managers.

Sometimes the overall objectives may seem to conflict directly with an organization's stated quality objectives. In short, they may appear muddled. An example is where there is a short-term (say, over the next year) objective of making significant improvements in the quality of products. The target could be to achieve a 33 percent improvement in customer satisfaction based on survey results. This may contrast with the same organization's longer-term business goal to achieve a significant (perhaps 50 percent) reduction in cost on the same product. Or it could be the other way around, with a short-term objective of 50 percent cost reduction with a long-term quality objective of improving customer satisfaction by 33 percent.

In such cases, the organization needs to go back to the basics and answer the question: "How do we make money in this business?" Recognizing the things that drive profitability can be a big aid in understanding how to align objectives. Figure 4.1 illustrates the idea that from an operational point of view most businesses make money by having less cost than revenue. It is easy to see that fewer problems in producing the product (due to defects, rework, extra operations, and the like) can reduce cost. It also can be true that better products and services can attract new customers, increase market share, and improve revenues. Thus better quality can improve both terms in our simple profit equation.

But we do not get those higher revenues and lower costs by just declaring that "we will improve the quality of everything we do." Such pronouncements alone do nothing to improve the organization because they are too general and do not address specific issues. Often they have the effect of dissipating energy and creating organizational frustration. Rather, we need to set objectives that enable us to focus on improving the things that are important. It is the role of top managers to "demuddle" these objectives. They need to understand how to use quality improvement to drive up revenue and drive down costs at the same time.

What action would top managers take in the organization with a short-term objective of 50 percent cost reduction with a stated quality objective of improving customer satisfaction by 33 percent? It would be their jobs to get

Figure 4.1   Relationship of quality and profitability.

the people in that organization to rapidly find process changes that reduce cost dramatically while *at the same time* improving the customer's perception of high quality. For example, if an organization is producing component parts in-house with high defect rates, it may be prudent to gather and analyze data to determine whether outsourcing the components to an expert supplier could both reduce cost and improve quality. To find changes like this, top managers need to define and measure the things that will drive this innovative behavior in the organization.

ALIGN MISSION, VISION, PLANS, AND POLICY

The importance of mission and vision was reviewed when we discussed business management principles in Chapter 1.

An organization's mission is a statement of the organization's reason to exist. It describes in high-level terms what the organization is. Clearly understanding what business the organization is in and how it succeeds in that business is crucial. Mission statements may reflect the way in which the organization behaves, how it pursues business opportunities, treats its people, or other information that is important to the understanding of the organization. Since mission statements express what the organization *is,* they seldom need to be changed.

An organization's vision describes a picture of the organization in the future. Understanding where the organization is going, or needs to go, is often as critical as understanding the current mission. Unlike the organization's mission, vision may need to change over time. Vision is developed by first developing a clear picture of the organization's current situation (sometimes called the "current reality") and then picturing what the organization needs to look like in the future. The process starts with top managers, who work out their picture of the organization's future and share it with the employees. Their objective should be to get employees to see how their vision relates to the top management's vision. This concept is sometimes called *shared vision.* Over time, shared vision should enable people in the organization to see the gap between their current actions and those needed to reach the vision.[1]

An organization's vision of the future may be quite different from its current situation. The organization may have vision of becoming something very different from what is described in its current mission statement. For example, the organization may have the vision of abandoning its current lines of business in favor of growth in other areas.

As described in Chapter 1, organizations should also develop a set of key values or principles to guide the actions and behaviors of the members of the organization.

In some cases, mission, vision, and key values can be developed independently of one another. Often they are interrelated. They should be the foundation for all that happens in the organization. They should be reflected in strategies and in all of the organization's policies, including quality policy. A clear understanding of the organization's mission, vision, and key values should precede the development of a strategic plan. Likewise, a clear understanding of mission, vision, key values, and current strategies is a prerequisite for drafting a quality policy. The quality policy should always display good alignment with an organization's mission, vision, key values, and strategies.

If the linkage shown in Figure 4.2 does not exist, there is little chance of aligning business objectives with quality objectives. Displaying this alignment in the words of mission and vision statements, policies, and so forth is a noble goal. But, the words need to represent real intentions of top managers. Fake alignment never works.

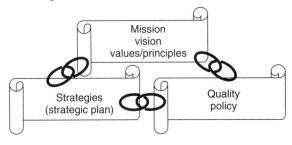

Figure 4.2   Alignment of mission, vision, values, strategies, and quality policy.

ALIGN THE ORGANIZATION'S OBJECTIVES

It is common to see two completely different sets of objectives. Overall business objectives and quality objectives often seem to conflict. This may be particularly true for organizations that are under extreme pressure to reduce costs but have objectives for "world-class" quality. Proper alignment of the quality objectives to the overall objectives of the business is a necessary step in achieving high levels of performance. This concept is shown in Figure 4.3.

Establishing overall business objectives is a natural function of top management. While ISO 9001 requires that top management establish the quality objectives, it is common practice for both the quality policy and the quality objectives to be drafted by a quality manager and approved by a top manager without much consideration of whether there is good alignment

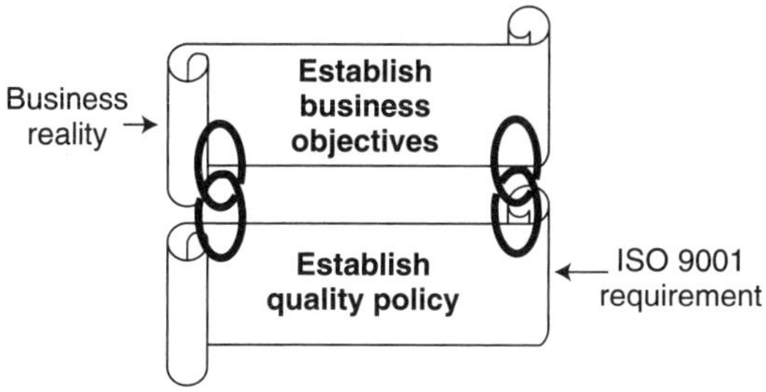

Figure 4.3 Alignment of business objectives and quality policy.

with the overall objectives of the organization. The question "What are quality objectives?" should not be asked in isolation. Rather, *the question should be, "What are the things related to quality that support our organizational objectives and what is our policy related to those things?"* So it is first necessary to align the quality policy with the organization's mission, strategic plans, business plans, and overall business objectives. Some of the considerations in developing objectives and quality policy include:

- Needs of customers in various market sectors
- Need for the organization to grow (or shrink) to suit market needs
- Market opportunities for current, new, and improved products
- Opportunities and needs for better technologies
- Needs of the organization's members for education, training, skills, and experience
- Capital needs for growth, new and improved products, and new processes
- Cash-flow needs to sustain operations
- Means to obtain required financing

Once business objectives and quality policy are aligned, it is appropriate to develop the quality objectives. This alignment is shown in Figure 4.4.

If the business objectives and quality policy are appropriate, it should be quite easy to develop aligned quality objectives to support them. This stage may also introduce needs that were not considered in earlier planning. For example, organizations that have a tradition of inward focus may not have even considered the needs of customers in developing their business objectives. This means that once the quality objectives have been devel-

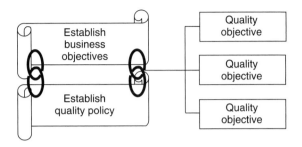

Figure 4.4 Alignment of quality objectives with business objectives and quality policy.

oped, they need to be checked against the business objectives and quality policy to test alignment. Objectives are needed to address both mission and vision. That is to say, we need to measure against both short and long term targets. Table 4.1 provides a format for testing this alignment.

Establishing this type of alignment may appear to be difficult. It isn't. In the Table 4.1 example, an organization needs to increase its margins on sales. There may be a business objective to increase margins by 10 percent over a one-year period. There might be several quality objectives that relate to this business objective. Two of them could be increasing customer satisfaction as measured by surveys by 35 percent to build customer loyalty while reducing quality failures by $50 million over the same year. Similar logic is used for objectives related to the vision.

Table 4.1 Test of alignment.

Components of mission and vision	Business objectives	Quality objectives
Mission • Provide XYZ service to meet customer needs at a price customers are willing to pay	**Year 2005** • 10% increase in profit margins • 15% reduction in operating cost	**Year 2005** • 35% improvement in customer satisfaction • Reduce quality failure costs by $50 million
Vision • Become the largest supplier of XYZ services in the country	**Years 2005–2008** • Expand service to one additional geographic area per year	**Years 2005–2008** • Introduce new service with 90% reduction in service complaints compared to last geographic expansion

MEASURE PROGRESS TOWARD OBJECTIVES AND THE BALANCED SCORECARD

Measurement is the most important activity for achieving improvement objectives. Without it, actions will lack focus and may even be directionless. Each objective should be measured. It is useful to capture these measures on a single balanced scorecard. The balanced scorecard process was discussed in Chapter 2. The measured objectives should address requirements of the organization's key stakeholders. The measures on the scorecard should be related to or the same as the measures of key process performance discussed in Chapter 5.

DEVELOP AND DEPLOY THE KEY DRIVERS OF PERFORMANCE

It is important to understand that we want to measure independent variables, not just response variables. The most important independent variables are the key drivers of performance. A simple example is shown in Figure 4.5.

Think about candy. If we want to control the sweetness of taste, we have two options for measurement: we can measure the taste itself or we can measure the amount of sugar we put in each batch. The amount of sugar is an independent variable, while the sweetness of taste is a response variable. The response variable gets sweeter as we add more sugar. Likewise, a business objective like "improve customer satisfaction as measured by surveys by 33 percent over two years" is a response variable. To drive the 33 percent improvement, we need to measure the independent variables that will cause customer perception to improve.

Measuring progress toward meeting the overall objectives is often not good enough, because they tend to be response variables. It is often neces-

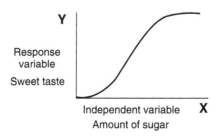

Figure 4.5   Response variables and independent variables.

sary to develop a small family of key measures that will drive performance. Targets should be set for each measure so that reaching the targets will result in meeting the organization's objectives. Selection of these key drivers is not a trivial task, and in most organizations the correct measures are not obvious. Their determination often has required several rounds of trial and error. But organizations should not just guess at what to measure, since this can lead to use of measures in which data collection is easiest or to a tendency to measure everything. Some analysis should be conducted to determine the key drivers.

To select the correct things to measure, we need to know what is important to customers and how those things relate to their perception of satisfaction. Sometimes simple tools like the cause-and-effect diagram are useful in defining these relationships. Consider gathering past data as a baseline and verifying that when the key driver you select changes, the response variable also changes as predicted. It is common for a single key driver (independent variable) to affect several of the objectives. When this happens, it is very good news because it can reduce the number of key drivers that need to be measured.

Many organizations have found that their objectives depend on removing wastes that are included in the cost of quality. For them, measuring cost of quality has become an important part of the key driver concept.

ACHIEVE ALIGNMENT OF THE LEADERS

In an ideal world, all leaders in the organization should have been participants in planning the business objectives, quality policy, and quality objectives. The leaders should be able to reach agreement or at least strong consensus during the planning process. In the real world, everyone's participation is often not feasible and the key leaders need to work hard to gain a consensus of the whole management team.

TOP MANAGEMENT REVIEW, ACTION, AND ONGOING ALIGNMENT

Top managers should regularly review progress on meeting the objectives. One way to structure this is to review the balanced scorecard measures first and then review key drivers that are not meeting targets. This may form a central part of a periodic operations review meeting. The result of these reviews should be action oriented. Examples include actions to realign resources as the situation changes, to establish projects to address problem areas, and to ensure coordination among the groups with joint responsibility for improvement projects. The purpose of reviews is not just to ensure coordination and take action, but also to ensure that alignment is maintained on the objectives.

MODIFY THE INFRASTRUCTURE TO INCLUDE IMPROVEMENT

Since most improvement is made project by project, it is important to have a mechanism to manage the projects. Some projects can be done by one person; others may require a cross-functional team with several subgroups. This concept scares people because it sounds like adding people or resources. We have been careful not to say "add infrastructure to manage the improvement process." The trick is to make these improvement activities a regular part of the work. It should not be something done by staff specialists (although they may participate or act as facilitators). If the objectives have been correctly set, meeting them is the most important thing the organization does. *It should not be considered extra work; it is the work.* In Chapter 6 we will deal further with the infrastructure needed to support continual improvement. In an organization that is just getting started, this support may need to extend to a small number of key teams working on significant issues related to the most important objectives. As time goes on, the infrastructure of the whole organization will need to be altered to embrace improvement as a key element of day-to-day work.

ALIGN PEOPLE—GET EVERYONE INVOLVED

Organizations tend to start real improvement activities at the top with teams driven by key executives as champions. The reason for this can be seen in Figure 4.6, which is an example of the measured costs of quality in a medium-size company. In this case, several big-ticket items are evident. It makes sense to put a high-level cross-functional team in charge of each and assign each team a vice president as champion.

Such a strategy makes a lot of sense. If the top four items were each addressed by a team and if each team were able to cut the failure costs in half, the organization would save over $42 million. After a few years of successful work by the four teams, the Pareto chart of these same opportunities might look more like Figure 4.7. There may remain sufficient opportunity

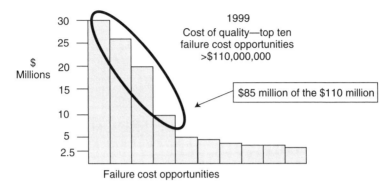

If you were the CEO, what would you do?

Figure 4.6   Use cost of quality to define key opportunities.

for a couple of the teams, with their high-level leadership, to continue their work, but the nature of the picture has changed. There are now many potential projects, and it will be necessary for most of them to be attacked by lower level champions and teams—there are just not enough vice presidents to go around.

It becomes necessary to look to the workforce to make the improvements. Figure 4.8 shows the breakdown of the opportunities represented by the third bar in Figure 4.7.

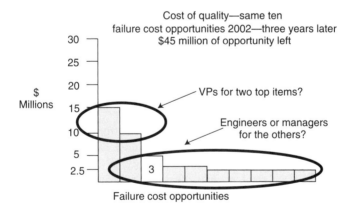

If you were the CEO, who would lead the teams now?

Figure 4.7   The key opportunities three years later.

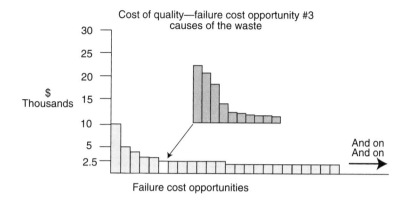

Figure 4.8 COQ analysis; now even our big opportunities have lots of components.

Even the scale has to be changed. Now many small projects must be analyzed to achieve the objectives. While it may be useful to involve all employees in improvement for other reasons, the compelling reason is that top management needs their help.

INFORMATION, EXPECTATIONS, BOUNDARY MANAGEMENT, AND ENVIRONMENT

Organizations need to start early in the process to think about aligning the working-level people as well as the top and middle managers. This involves action on four fronts:

- **Information sharing**—Share not only objectives but also the information, measures, and data that are needed to understand opportunities and carry out improvement projects.

- **Changing expectations**—Make it clear that the expectations of the organization have changed. It is no longer sufficient to just do your job; you must also learn how to improve it.

- **Boundary management**—Set the boundaries of action for all levels in the organization. Each individual should be innovative and make improvements, but you do not want chaos!

- **Providing a supportive environment**—Top and middle managers will need to start behaving in ways that encourage input from everyone. It is necessary to understand how to gain the trust of employees.

Information and data are power. It is common for managers to hold the numbers close to the chest and share only the information that workers need to do specific tasks. In such cases workers have a hard time relating their own performance to the overall results of the organization. It is important to learn which information is helpful to the workforce and to find an appropriate way to share it. To the extent that a piece of information or data would improve a worker's ability to make correct decisions, solve problems, and improve performance, it should be shared. Some information, such as current financial results, overall customer satisfaction, and other high-level data, is often important as background. It may explain why certain of an organization's objectives have been established. Other information should enable workers to understand how they contribute to overall performance.

Each employee or work team should understand how the objectives apply in their area and should know how they can contribute to achieving them. *Remember that what gets measured gets done.* Measuring the things that drive performance improvement is important, but it is more important to eliminate measures that drive performance in the wrong direction. If the key measure of performance is the speed with which work is done and if speed causes mistakes, it does little good to tell the workers to produce no defects. They will do what is measured: work fast!

This leads to expectations. Rewording an old saying, we come up with, "If you always expect what you always expected, you will always get what you always got." There is no getting around it; clear understanding of expectations is a must. There are two components of this concept:

1. It is not acceptable to have more than one standard for a product or process. People should *know* how performance is to be measured, and we should never change those measures after the fact. We need to put in the past the times when we shipped product at month's end that would have been scrapped a few days earlier. Double standards need to go away.

2. We should set proper targets for improvement. There is a myth that targets should always be "achievable" or "reasonable." Nothing could be further from reality. *More often than not, the macro-objectives that the organization sets are imposed by the external market, by customers, or even by the banker.* Often we don't get to decide how "good" the customers want our products or services to be. Our goals should reflect real needs. Often that means that when we set the targets, we do not yet know how we will meet them. This is a good-news, bad-news situation. The bad news is we don't know how to hit our targets. The good news is that to be successful we will have to

learn how to change our processes and that learning is the real
fun of improvement. Learning is also a key principle in the
Japanese Technical Report 00005, mentioned in Chapter 1.

Clear boundaries need to be established for individual and team action.
Those boundaries need to be understood by all, and they need to make
sense. If they are too restrictive, everyone will know it and performance will
suffer. If they are too loose, the organization risks chaos. As the organization
matures, creating a supportive environment becomes *the* job of middle managers, not just one of their jobs.

Establishing a supportive environment is easier than most people think.
This means that we need to treat all of our employees fairly and support
them in doing and improving their jobs. It is important to recognize the dis-
tinction between the things in your organization that provide direct or indirect support for doing and improving work and those things that are just
nice for the employees to have. For example, having a space in the operations area where teams can meet for solving problems may be a key to performance improvements. Providing a sensible reward and recognition
structure may be important to sustaining the improvement efforts. Having
an exercise facility in the plant may have a far less direct role in improving
performance. Exercise facilities and other amenities can be good for
employee performance, but it is important to understand which of these support mechanisms should be retained when it comes time to cut the budget!

Creating a supportive environment has another aspect—that of employee
attitude toward improvement.

As Figure 4.9 illustrates, it is natural for some people to be more supportive than others of the new objectives and emphasis on improvement.
The curve may not actually be normal and the proportions of followers,
naysayers, and innovators may be different if they were measured, but in
most organizations, all three types of people are recognizable. Managers
need to start getting full alignment of the workforce by focusing on those

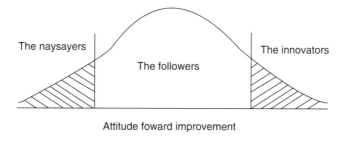

Figure 4.9   Employee attitudes toward improvement.

who are most ready to accept change. This means identifying the innovators among the workforce. It means finding those who will be willing to lead the change and those who will be the inhibitors. If managers think through which categories their people fall into, they may gain insight as to how to build a critical mass of workers who are aligned with the organization's objectives.

ORGANIZATIONAL CULTURE AND BEHAVIOR

An organization's culture is the combined knowledge, beliefs, and behaviors that are held by the organization's members. People often talk about changing the culture of an organization, and over time every organization's culture does change. It is, however, very difficult to change the "belief" component of culture. Leaders can provide new knowledge and can expect different behaviors. As knowledge expands and behaviors change, the belief set and thus the culture may be altered.

You often hear people say things like, "We need to change the culture of our organization," or even "Our culture is so messed up, we could never do that." It is true that each organization has its own unique culture. That organizational culture is the result of many things. It may have been shaped by the attitude of the organization's founder, molded by the history of the industry, shaped by years of consistent training, or driven to lethargy by measurements that are irrelevant to real performance. Making direct changes in culture is very difficult. If the culture is not right, it is best changed by indirect action such as forcing a change in behaviors. As behaviors change over time, the culture will change so the new behaviors become part of the new culture. The recommendations of this chapter are intended to provide insight into some of the things you can consider doing to change behaviors. If you focus on getting the behavior right, the cultural habits will change for the better over time.

WHAT CAN I DO NOW?

To address questions related to the alignment of all functions and personnel in the organization, ask and answer the following questions about your organization:

- In your organization, how are objectives set?
- Are objectives derived from the vision and mission of the organization, and do they support achievement of both?

- Are there objectives in place that, when achieved, will result in organizational compliance with the words in the quality policy?

- Are the objectives assigned throughout the organization so that everyone feels as though they have a contribution to make to the satisfaction of our customers, not just doing a job in isolation?

- Does your organization measure indicators of performance in areas that support making the business plan, the vision, the mission, and the quality policy a reality?

- Does your organization's culture support innovation, learning, and improvement? If not, what behaviors need to be changed and what action should be taken?

Answers to these questions should guide projects to address gaps between current performance and the behaviors needed to achieve the business vision and mission and quality policy.

5

Use Process Management Techniques

"The one fact that I would cry from every housetop is this:
the Good Life is waiting for us—here and now! . . .
At this very moment we have the necessary techniques,
both material and psychological, to create a full
and satisfying life for everyone."

Burrhus Frederich Skinner
Walden II (1948), Chapter 23

Process management is one of the best ways to focus the organization's activities on meeting quality and business objectives. Let's think in terms of a small business that needs a bank loan to grow. What does the banker demand in terms of a business plan? There are lots of ways for the banker to say it, but the basic question is, "How will your processes yield enough money to pay back the loan and interest on time?" The basic issue is not just results; it is how you will manage the process to consistently achieve the desired results.

This chapter will discuss the basics of process management. First it will review the concept of the system approach to management and systems thinking. The chapter will also cover process ownership and process champions for key processes, understanding key processes, identification of customers and suppliers for each key process, process measurement and process mapping, analysis and improvement of processes, implementation of process changes, process measurement and improvement, and the role of top managers. This fits within a larger context of other important considerations in quality management system development, as shown in Figure 5.1.

How does this differ from what is done during many ISO 9000 implementations? Many organizations have been encouraged to document what is being done now and rigorously comply with the documentation. The old

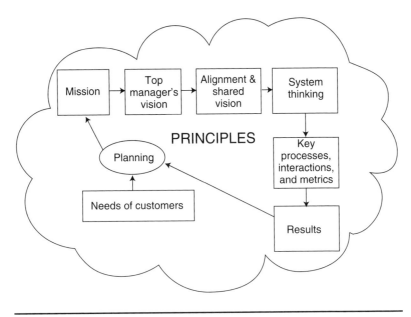

Figure 5.1 Considerations in quality management system development.

saw has been "say what you do; do what you say." There are four profound difficulties with that approach:

1. It institutionalizes practices that have developed over time. Often these practices have not been well thought out, and most important, this approach tends to ignore the organization's objectives. Documenting what is being done means that the results currently being obtained will continue. Often, practices develop because of a pressing need or identified problem. Such practices may have been developed in isolation without careful consideration of their impact on other activities in the process. If all the organization wants is stability and the results achieved in the past are good enough for the future, perhaps the old way is good enough. But for most organizations, times and requirements change; new approaches are needed. There is a need to ensure that the documented management system is focused on achieving the organization's objectives.

2. It tends to place the same emphasis on each process. There seems to be the assumption that all organizations must be good at every process. Nothing could be further from the truth. In practice, organizations need to determine those processes that are important to meeting their objectives and customer require-

ments. Management systems that lack this clear focus on the key processes are often perceived as bureaucratic exercises without value. Also, the limited resources of the organization must be allocated carefully, with priority attention to the most significant or pressing issues.

3. It may ignore process interactions. It is common for difficulties to occur at the interfaces between processes. If processes are developed in isolation, interactions are not considered. This can result in suboptimization and unintended consequences elsewhere in the system.

4. It may ignore multiple interactions with customers caused by multiple customer contact points. There may also be interactions with customers that are needed but not recognized. Many suppliers have multiple contacts with customers. There are often direct links between customer engineering and supplier engineering, customer purchasing and supplier sales, customer scheduling and supplier production, customer quality and supplier quality assurance. The supplier that manages each of these interfaces separately without coordinating the interactions between its associated internal processes is asking for trouble.

Implementation of ISO 9001 in the "say what you do; do what you say" manner may yield a certificate, but it often does not build an effective and efficient management system capable of continual improvement.

SYSTEM APPROACH TO MANAGEMENT AND SYSTEMS THINKING

It is best to manage the system, not just the individual processes. Recall the operational management principle from Chapter 1: "Manage a system of interrelated processes—managing activities and resources together as a process improves the ability to meet process output needs. Managing the interactions among the processes as a system enables the organization to be more effective and efficient at meeting objectives."

ISO 9001 has a requirement that the organization identify not only the processes of the quality management system but also the interactions among those processes. So the system approach is basic to ISO 9001. Indeed, this holistic concept of managing the system of processes with associated resources to achieve objectives is central to all successful system implementations.

But systems thinking is much more. Peter M. Senge, in his best-selling book *The Fifth Discipline,* described it this way: "Systems thinking is a discipline for seeing wholes. It is a framework for seeing interrelationships rather than things, for seeing patterns of change rather than static 'snapshots.' " [1]

In managing individual processes we tend to look for direct linear cause-and-effect relationships. In the ideal process, we can measure and control a small number of independent variables to control the behavior of outputs (response variables). Managing the system is quite different. *Systems thinking teaches us to look at interactions rather than searching for direct cause and effect relationships.*

Quality professionals need to become masters of "systems thinking." Senge defined 11 "laws" of systems thinking.[2] He called them "the laws of the fifth discipline." The laws are:

1. "Today's problems come from yesterday's solutions."

2. "The harder you push, the harder the system pushes back."

3. "Behavior grows better before it grows worse."

4. "The easy way out usually leads back in."

5. "The cure can be worse than the disease."

6. "Faster is slower."

7. "Cause and effect are not closely related in time and space."

8. "Small changes can produce big results—but the areas for high leverage are often the least obvious."

9. "You can have your cake and eat it too—but not at once."

10. "Dividing an elephant in half does not produce two small elephants."

11. "There is no blame."

We have all seen the truth of these in our business lives. Think carefully about laws 2, 7, and 8. It is our experience that when we try to make positive changes the whole system tends to push back. It is also unfortunate that we often don't see the real effect of a change until long after it was made. Finding the small changes that have big positive results is always difficult, but most of us have seen small changes make huge differences in results. We have often seen quality improvement proposals that were resisted by the system and eventually turned into cost reductions that helped make short-term financial numbers. The resulting rise in warranty costs a year later are blamed on "those quality guys who didn't control the parts," while the cost reduction story is long forgotten. So much for "no blame!"

The point is that if the managers of such situations can be made to see the business as a system, they will be able to look for the best overall result, not just grab the quick money and hope there will be no adverse consequences.

It can be argued that the need for systems thinking is great because organizations are faced with increased complexity.[3] Senge talks about two kinds of complexity: detail complexity, where we are faced with more and more details in all aspects of life, and dynamic complexity, where the relationship between cause and effect may be obscure. "The real leverage in most management situations lies in understanding dynamic complexity, not detail complexity."[4]

BASICS OF PROCESS MANAGEMENT

The concept of process management is simple: View the organization as a collection of interrelated processes all having the purpose of achieving the organization's objectives. At the simplest level, all of the work of the organization occurs as part of a process. A process is defined in ISO 9000:2000 as a "set of interrelated or interacting activities which transforms inputs into outputs." Figure 5.2 illustrates this simple concept.

Processes must be supported with resources. A person or a group of people can conduct each process activity. Sometimes, whole departments are established to do a single activity. The people who work within the process use other types of resources to make the transformation possible. These resources may include:

- Equipment such as production equipment, telephones, computers, robots, and transportation equipment

- Data, information, and software to manipulate the information and data

- Workspace and associated support items such as air conditioning, desks, and tables

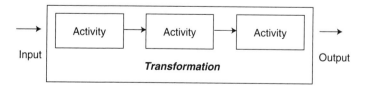

Figure 5.2   Process: set of interrelated or interacting activities that transforms inputs into outputs.

Processes are also controlled by a variety of human, mechanical, and electronic means. Some examples of control mechanisms include:

- Normal day-to-day supervision

- Automated control systems that adjust the process when it drifts from established values

- Inspection of the work using criteria that have been established in the context of customer needs

- Foolproofing devices to prevent the process from producing items that do not meet established rules

Resources and controls can be viewed as supporting the process as illustrated in Figure 5.3.

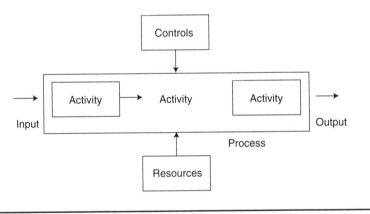

Figure 5.3   Processes are supported by resources and controls.

MANAGE THE SYSTEM

The process concept is a simple one. If your organization had only one key process (and some organizations do), process management would be quite simple. But most organizations have a number of key processes and also have supporting processes without which the key processes could not operate.

These processes interact with one another to form a system. Organizations should be seeking to develop that system so that it more effectively and efficiently meets the needs of customers and achieves the organization's objectives. Figure 5.4 illustrates the concept of a system of interrelated processes, continually improved and driven by top managers, with a focus on meeting objectives and satisfying customer needs.

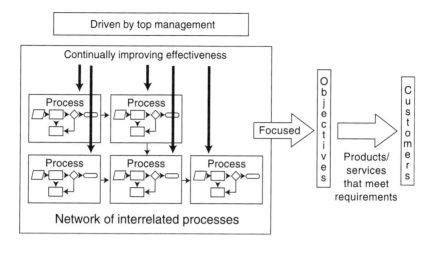

Figure 5.4 System: family of well-managed processes.

Many organizations expend significant resources on such activities as flowcharting and get little real benefit. Often this is because they have not addressed the true meaning of process management. An understanding of process management begins with an enigmatic dichotomy (a problem that seems intractable and has components that seem to be mutually exclusive). There seems to be an enigma in that the problem of getting benefits seems insolvable. The problem seems hard to solve because it is a dichotomy:

- To benefit from the process management concept, we must first understand the organization's key drivers of performance.

- To understand the important drivers of performance, we must understand the key processes.

This situation is made more complex because understanding how results are achieved also requires us to understand the interactions between the processes.

Chapter 4 discusses development and deployment of key drivers of performance. It indicates that determination of the correct key drivers may require several rounds of trial and error. While the process is lengthy, its potential rewards are great. The worst thing to do is to never start!

We can start by asking several questions:

- How does the organization make money and satisfy customer requirements?

- Which processes have interfaces with the organization's customers?

- What processes are involved in satisfying customer requirements and adding value?

- What processes most affect the organization's ability to meet key driver targets?

- What supporting processes appear in the interrelationships that are critical to success?

- What are the interrelationships among these processes?

From the answers to these questions, distill out the processes that appear to be the keys to satisfying customers and making money. Then look at how these processes can be measured. We may not yet know the true key driver measures of performance, but the processes you identify should align with the list of key drivers you developed when you read Chapter 4.

The various process interrelationships need to be understood. It is also smart to identify the other necessary supporting processes and their interaction with the key processes. Start by understanding the *basics* of how the organization works. Start at a high level; don't get bogged down in details.

- Map the overall (high-level) value stream for the organization.

- Map overall (high-level) flow of managerial, administrative, and supporting processes.

- Map the *basic* interactions among the processes.

- Understand the interactions with the customer and the processes that are keys to meeting customer requirements.

The basic concept of process management is to measure, manage, and improve the key processes and their interrelationships so that overall business performance is improved.

You will need to deal with situations in which there are more than one process that have interfaces with the organization's customers. For example, product design requirements may enter the organization's design process from a customer engineering department, while needed volumes may come to the organization's order input process from the customer's enterprise resource planning (ERP) system output. In such cases, linkages between the internal design process and the order entry system need to be recognized and managed.

PROCESS CHAMPIONS, PROCESS OWNERSHIP, AND PROCESS TEAMS

Once the key processes have been identified and their interactions understood, it is time to act. There is a temptation to try to make what appear to be obvious improvements. This can be a big mistake, because the processes involve people and people will always resist change. Recall Senge's laws of the fifth discipline, in particular, law number 2.

Our next action is not making immediate improvements, but rather overcoming objections to improvement and the inevitable changes required. Alignment, covered in Chapter 3, is now critical. We need to think through how we can develop the changes in a way that will maximize our success in driving improvement of our key processes. The nature of the approach depends on such things as the size of the organization, its culture, the nature of its key processes, and its improvement objectives. The most important aspect of this is involvement of the right people in the process management activities. It is best to assign a member of the top management as a *process champion* for each key process. The champion acts as the link between those doing the process management work and the senior executive team. Inevitably resource or cooperation issues will surface. When this happens, the process owner or process team leader can always communicate to top management through the champion. A process champion should have sufficient interest in the success of the process in achieving business performance improvement that he or she will be an active champion. Although it may be best to assign the executive who has the greatest organizational influence over the process, this is not always the best approach. In cases where there is a significant spirit of cooperation among the senior executives, the champion need not be responsible for all or part of the process. It is useful to weigh the pros and cons of the individual senior leaders in developing process champion assignments. To the extent possible, each senior executive should be assigned as champion of one process and no senior executive should be left out.

The next action needs to be the assignment of process owners who will serve as team leaders for each process. It is best to first identify what parts of the organization are involved in each process. It is useful to develop a chart showing the key and support processes and the departments or groups involved in each. Figure 5.5 illustrates such a chart. In many cases, it is important to select a key manager from the most affected department as the process owner. That person will need to serve as team leader for the process management work and will need to lead a cross-functional team made up of people from each affected department. The individual selected should be a senior manager of the most affected department but not necessarily the department head. It is more important that the individual selected have good team leadership skills and the ability to communicate at all levels than it is to have the most senior manager. For some processes, the process owner role may be a part-time assignment; for the key processes, the job may, initially at least, be a full-time assignment, so careful selection is imperative.

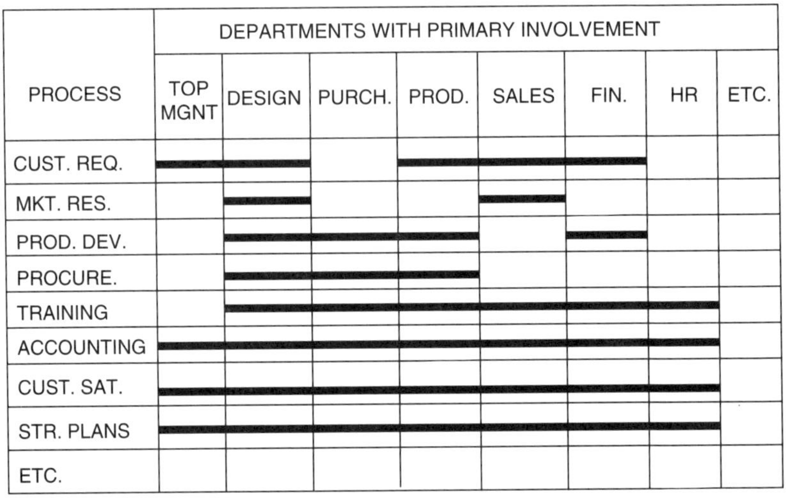

PROCESS	DEPARTMENTS WITH PRIMARY INVOLVEMENT							
	TOP MGNT	DESIGN	PURCH.	PROD.	SALES	FIN.	HR	ETC.
CUST. REQ.	▬			▬	▬			
MKT. RES.		▬			▬			
PROD. DEV.		▬	▬	▬		▬		
PROCURE.		▬	▬	▬				
TRAINING		▬	▬	▬	▬	▬	▬	▬
ACCOUNTING	▬	▬	▬	▬	▬	▬	▬	
CUST. SAT.	▬	▬	▬	▬	▬	▬	▬	
STR. PLANS	▬	▬	▬	▬	▬	▬	▬	
ETC.								

Figure 5.5 Departments involved in each process.

Let's look at an example of the logic that could develop from a chart like Figure 5.5. First, every department is involved in the accounting process, and since Finance would seem to be the clear process leader, it could be expected that the process owner for the accounting process would come from that function. Figure 5.5 also shows that Top Management, Design, Production, Sales, and Finance are all involved in determination of customers' requirements. After some thought, it might be determined that the Design and Sales departments have most of the accountabilities in determining customers' requirements, while Finance has a secondary but important role. The process owner for this process could thus come from Design or Sales. But consider the individuals involved. It may be that Design and Sales are often at each other's throats about requirements. If the logical candidates from Design and Sales are not the sort of people who can see the other side of an issue and work toward consensus, an individual from Finance who has those traits may be a better choice. If determination of customer requirements is a key process for the organization and accounting is a stable support process, it may be more important for our accounting candidate to work on the customer requirements process.

It is the job of the process champion to make certain that the process management team is established. The champion should make certain that the team has the right members and should support the process owner by attending initial meetings and conducting progress reviews as the team's work proceeds. An initial activity of the team is to establish a clear relationship between the process and the key driver objectives, develop a charter, and obtain charter approval. The team will also need to decide how to deal with coordination of process interactions with the other teams. The champion should be involved in these early activities to ensure alignment of objectives. Perhaps the most important early activity is establishing the team charter. There are several important steps and items to consider. It is usually best if the champion first writes down the team's basic assignment. The assignment can form the basis for the charter. At its first meeting the team should discuss the assignment and develop an initial list of actions required to accomplish it. Consider including in the charter such items as:

- A revised assignment statement

- A list of objectives for the project

- A set of measures to tell when the project is completed and whether it met its objectives

- A basic description of how the project will be carried out, including key actions

- A schedule with mileposts

The charter should be approved by the champion and updated as necessary during the project.

SIPOC—IDENTIFY CUSTOMERS AND SUPPLIERS FOR EACH KEY PROCESS

The basic SIPOC idea (suppliers, inputs, process, outputs, and customers) is illustrated in Figure 5.6. There is a temptation to dive right in and start working on the process and its activities. Successful teams resist this temptation. Yielding to it can be fatal to the project. Remember Senge's sixth law: "Faster is slower." Each process team needs to first determine key customers and outputs. Next it needs to identify suppliers and inputs. In doing this, the team needs to communicate with customers who receive the output and suppliers who provide the inputs. All of this should be done before attacking the process itself.

The first step is to identify what customers need from the process in the form of outcomes. This information needs to come from direct discussion with the customer. The outputs of the process need to match the customers' expected outcomes. The next step is to gain agreement with those customers on how to measure these outputs. Figure 5.7 illustrates one way that the resulting information can be displayed. In this example, the process is product design and the team has reached agreement with an

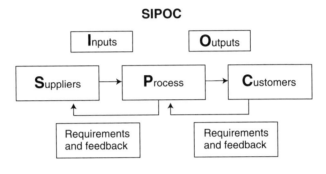

SIPOC

Figure 5.6   SIPOC—suppliers provide inputs, which the process transforms into outputs for customers.

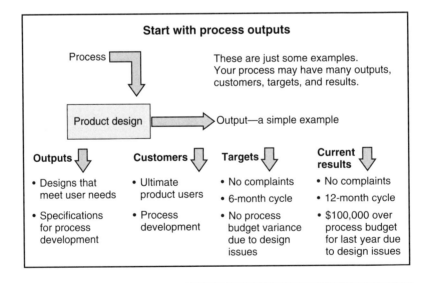

Figure 5.7   Identify customers and agree on measures of process outputs.

internal customer (process engineering) on its requirements. Since the other major customer of the process is the ultimate user of the product, the results of customer surveys and focus groups were used to develop an understanding of customer requirements as an input to the specification of the product requirements.

In the example, both the targets and current results are identified. It is important to establish how well the current process is doing to meet the customer requirements. Targets that are not being met can be used to identify opportunities for process improvement. In developing the targets, consideration should be given to future as well as current needs.

The process team's next step is to identify input requirements to the process and to reach agreement with the suppliers on how the inputs are to be measured. Figure 5.8 illustrates the result for the product design process.

In our example, the team follows the same process used for determining customers and output requirements. The members determine the inputs, talk with the suppliers, determine current targets, and measure current performance for process inputs. In developing the targets, the team should consider future as well as current needs. The team now has an initial set of process inputs, measures of performance, current level of performance, and targets.

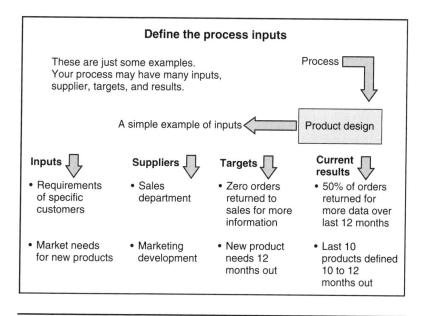

Figure 5.8   Identify suppliers and agree on measures of process inputs.

Each team should now validate overall process measures and targets. The basic question is, "If the targets are met, will this result in the desired impact on the key driver(s)?" At some point, the process owners collectively should determine what targets need to be changed to ensure that the organization's quality and business objectives will be met.

RESOURCES AND CONTROLS

Defining and measuring process inputs and outputs enables the team to understand some of the most important process interactions. But interfaces with other value chain processes may not be the only interactions that need to be understood and managed. The team may need to look at interactions with processes that provide controls and resources. Recall that Figure 5.3 illustrates that a process is made up of activities that transform inputs into outputs, but most processes need resources and controls. There may be important interactions with other processes that provide these resources and controls. Where this is the case, the team should consider defining the measures, targets, and current performance for these supporting inputs.

OTHER PROCESS INTERACTIONS

Once the process inputs and outputs have been defined, it is worthwhile to step back and ask, "Have we covered all of the process interactions?" Often the answer is no. In the design process discussed above, we see that customer design requirements come from the sales department; that is the formal route. But we may find that once a contract has been signed, there is direct communication between the customer's engineering and our organization's designers. This direct contact needs to be captured and provided for—not only in this process, but also in others that may be affected. For example, a customer comment on a design submittal may cause a design change that affects the manufacturing process. In practice, suppliers often have many processes with direct interaction with their customers. Careful consideration is needed in managing internal process interactions where there are multiple customer contact points. Figure 5.9 illustrates that these interactions can be complex. And there are interactions with internal support processes that should not be ignored. Sometimes these are the most important of all. For example, in the design process, a critical interaction may be with the human resources hiring process to ensure that the organization hires competent design engineers.

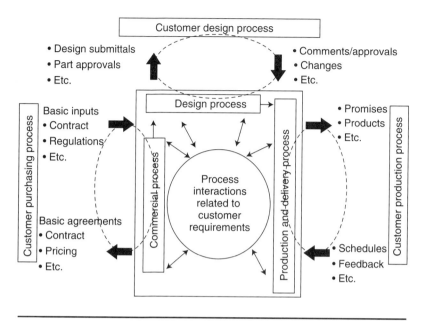

Figure 5.9 Manage internal interactions where there are multiple customer interfaces.

It can easily be seen that a small change at one interaction could have a big affect on another part of the system and that this effect is often remote in time and space from the cause (Senge's seventh law of "systems thinking"). Remember that cause-and-effect relationships are often very subtle!

The interactions are numerous and complex. Simplification is important. One technique is to use simple tables. The team assigned to each process records the inputs and outputs along with process activities in a table, such as that shown in Table 5.1.

Table 5.1 Process interactions for a single process.

Process name		
Inputs	Process activities	Outputs
• Input 1 • Input 2 • Input 3 • Etc.	• Activity 1 • Activity 2 • Activity 3 • Etc.	• Output 1 • Output 2 • Output 3 • Etc.
Input measures • Input 1 measure • Input 2 measure • Input 3 measure • Etc.	Process measures • Meaure 1 • Meaure 2 • Meaure 3 • Etc.	Output measures • Output 1 measure • Output 2 measure • Output 3 measure • Etc.

Table 5.2   Process interactions of the whole system.

	Process A	Process B	Process C	External customers & suppliers
Process A	Activities of process A	A's inputs to B	A's inputs to C	A's inputs to external customers & suppliers
Process B	B's inputs to A	Activities of process B	B's inputs to C	B's inputs to external customers & suppliers
Process C	C's inputs to A	C's inputs to B	Activities of process C	C's inputs to external customers & suppliers
External customers & suppliers	Customers' & suppliers' inputs to A	Customers' & suppliers' inputs to B	Customers' & suppliers' inputs to C	

After each process has been analyzed this way, a master table such as the one shown in Table 5.2 can be developed to cross-check the work. The table shows the important process activities and the more important interactions on one page.

FLOWCHART OF THE PROCESS

The next step in process management is to create a flowchart of the process activities. This work is often best done by the personnel who work in the process. Flowcharting enables us to understand the activities in the process and how they relate to each other. There are several software packages available to aid in the work and many books that discuss how to do it, so we won't describe the technique in detail.[5] There are, however, several important points to remember:

- Start by charting the process as it is now—not the way you think it should be. Before we make improvements, it is important to understand how things are done now.

- Include detail. You can always simplify your chart later, but if you leave out critical steps or activities that take place infrequently you may miss significant opportunities to improve process performance.

- Involve the people who work in the process in the initial flowcharting.

- Include key information on the chart such as who performs each activity. Be as specific as possible.

- Include available data on each activity such as how well the activity is performed, cycle times, volumes, inventories at each activity, and so forth. At this stage it may not be desirable to perform measurement activities, but inclusion of data that are available can be helpful.

- Remember that most processes flow across functional lines. Do not make the mistake of restricting your chart to the activities that are conducted in one function alone, since this can lead to suboptimization by function.

A flowchart is created to provide *clarity* of process understanding. This means that you should focus on achieving clear process understanding and not on making the chart look good or on following a specific flowcharting technique. The best initial flowcharts look messy, have notes and data all over them, and are hard for those not involved in their preparation to interpret. Remember, the purpose of the initial flowchart is to provide the team with process understanding that can be used for analysis and process improvement. Later, after the analysis and improvement phase and as part of process documentation, simplified charts can be prepared.

Types of Processes

The tools used for process analysis and improvement can be applied to a wide variety of processes. This may not be obvious, however, since people who work in one type of process may not be able to see how techniques used for other types of process can be applied in their case. There are also situations where the tools used for one type of process are not appropriate for others. In many cases, the difference is in the types of activities within the process. For example, consider the following:

- **Creative, administrative, managerial processes—** characterized by activities such as thinking, writing, decision making, talking, reading

- **Manual labor and service processes**—loading, check cashing, hotel check-in, cleaning, manual assembly

- **Discrete mechanical processes**—characterized by activities like machining, operating construction equipment, operating test equipment

- **Continuous flow processes**—chemical processing, papermaking

Table 5.3   Types of processes.

Process	Typical characteristic activities	Resource requirements	Typical controls
Creative, administrative, managerial	Thinking Writing Decision making Talking Reading Project management	People intensive	Supervision Audits Peer reviews
Manual labor and service	Loading Check cashing Hotel check-in Cleaning Manual assembly	People intensive	Supervision Audits Inspection Automated test
Discrete mechanical	Machining Operating construction equipment Operating test equipment	Capital and people intensive	Inspection SPC Supervision Fool-proofing Process auditing Automated test
Continuous flow	Chemical processing Papermaking Water treatment	Capital intensive	Automated control Continuous monitoring

Table 5.3 illustrates some of the differences in the activities, resources, and typical controls for these four types of processes.

Recognizing that different types of processes have different characteristics can help in understanding how to analyze each type. While the basics of process analysis apply to all types, the appropriate analytical tools to use may vary.

Analyze the Value Stream

Value-stream mapping has become a valuable tool for analyzing the entire value stream for a product or even for a whole business. In their book *Value Stream Management: Eight Steps to Planning, Mapping, and Sustaining Lean Improvements,* Don Tapping, Tom Luyster, and Tom Shuker state: "Because a value stream map gives a visual representation of material and information flow for a product family (value stream), it is indispensable as a tool for visually managing process improvements. To improve a process you must first observe and understand it."[6] It is appropriate to use this technique when we deal with improving the management system, but it is particularly useful for analyzing manufacturing value streams to plan implementation of lean manufacturing. There are three basic questions that should be considered:

1. Does the outcome of the process or activity add value? To answer this yes, the outcome must be a part of a stream of events that cause the customer to buy the product or service. In this case, the outcome is not just a necessity; it adds value. If the answer is an honest yes, the organization must continue to provide the outcome. The process or activity remains a candidate for reengineering, simplification, combination, or other improvement. Examples of value-adding activities might be stamping an automobile part or drawing money out of a bank account. In both cases, the outcome can be done in different ways. To get the money from the bank in the past you had to go to the teller and make a withdrawal. But the banking industry changed the process to allow you to access your account at ATMs located almost anywhere. In this example, the outcome is retained but the process has been changed significantly. If the answer to question one is no, the outcome should be covered by either question two or three.

2. Does the outcome of the process or activity have to exist for the value stream to work? Even if the outcome of the process or activity does not add value, it may still be unavoidable. For example, many businesses must receive customer orders before providing products or services. The outcome is the agreement of the customer to buy the organization's product or to use its service. While the outcome may be needed, the specific process may be ripe for improvement.

3. Is the outcome not needed at all? This is the case where eliminating the activity would not affect the value stream. Such activities as acceptance inspection are often cited as examples. In many cases, elimination of an inspection step has no effect except to lower cost and possibly improve quality by eliminating handling.

One of the keys to success with value-stream analysis is to think about the process outcome first. If the outcome is not needed, the whole process is wasteful. If the outcome is necessary but does not add value, look for ways to simplify the process or to change the entire value stream to eliminate the need for the outcome or to make the outcome an automatic result of another process. Foolproofing and Poka Yoke devices are examples of the concept. They tend to embed the inspection process in the production process by making mistakes impossible.

At the system level, we should think about processes this way, and value-stream mapping can be used as a tool to identify areas where lean production techniques should be considered. At the process level, questions like these should be asked about each activity. The result should be a list of potential opportunities for improvement.

PROCESS ANALYSIS AND IMPROVEMENT

The flowchart, along with the process inputs, outputs, measures, and targets, should now be analyzed to find opportunities for improvement. The following sections of this chapter will discuss a number of techniques for determining and acting on process improvement opportunities.

Process Benchmarking

It is always good to learn from others, and benchmarking is a useful tool for learning different and perhaps better ways of operating a process. The best time to conduct a benchmarking study for a process is when you have a complete understanding of how your own process works and what your own measurable process results are. In most cases, there is little value in benchmarking done before this understanding has been achieved. Some have called such misadventures "industrial tourism." Much has been written on benchmarking, so we will only outline the process.[7]

Benchmarking involves determining best-in-class performance for a process. The organization conducting the benchmarking study performs literature research to determine process performance levels in their own and in other industries. Surveys may be conducted to gather data from a broad group of organizations that operate the process. Often other organizations are approached with the proposal that process data and techniques be shared. This may be easy for organizations that have the same process but are in a different industry. Not all organizations are willing to be benchmarking partners and, in all cases, care is needed to protect the information obtained. The basic objective is to obtain three types of information:

- Data to provide an understanding of how your organization's process stacks up against the best

- Process flows and activities that are key to the achievement of the benchmark results

- Key supporting processes (such as training) and cultural environment (such as a recognition scheme), without which the benchmark results could not be achieved

It is not uncommon to find that the benchmark process results are a lot better than one's own for the same process. It is common to find that certain supporting processes and cultural characteristics are needed to achieve the superior results. Well-prepared reports of benchmarking studies can be valuable in identifying opportunities for process improvement. If the benchmark results are very much better than your own, it may be that your process targets need to be even more aggressive.

Should We Reengineer?

If the process, activity, or operation does not meet output targets, there is a temptation to take out a sheet of paper and reengineer the process. If the current process has never been able to meet its current targets or if it employs technology or methods that are inherently incapable of meeting current or future needs, then such reengineering may well be appropriate. Often the process has a number of internal problems that keep it from reaching the level of performance that we expected. In such cases, *reengineering* may not be as cost effective as defining and solving those problems.

Look for Obvious Inefficiencies or Disconnects

Very often process improvement opportunities become obvious from a review of process maps. Significant improvements are sometimes possible, so it is appropriate to ask such questions as:

- Are there obvious inefficiencies or disconnects (for example, things going to the wrong place, or obvious causes of defects) in the process?
- Do we need to know the cause of these inefficiencies in order to correct them? Do we already know what to do?
  - –If we already know how to correct these issues, we should do so!
  - –If we find we need to know the causes to correct them, we will need to determine if the cost of determining the cause is worth the improvement that will be gained by eliminating the problem.
- Is this one of the organization's key processes?

Find and Solve Process Problems

We need to ask basic questions about the process and decide how to proceed. We will need to know such things as:

- Does it meet our expected output targets?

- Are there problems that cause the process to miss targets?

- If not, do data indicate the process is stable and in control?

- Do we know the measures of activities within the process that if changed would improve our output?

Figure 5.10 illustrates a thought process to consider when a process does not meet a target. First we ask ourselves whether meeting the target is really necessary. It is amazing how often the real answer is a resounding, "No, we don't really need that." Or, "If other things are changed, the target becomes irrelevant."

If the target cannot be changed, we should think about the process's basic capability. If, for example, we were to improve the process by solving its current problems, would it be capable of meeting the target? It may be useful to conduct a brainstorming session with the people who work in and around the process. Often an honest assessment of this question yields a plentiful list of problems that keep the process from meeting its targets. If solutions to these problems are implemented, the targeted results may be achieved. If this is the case, some testing of possible causes and remedies may validate that the problem-solving approach is best. If the problems are

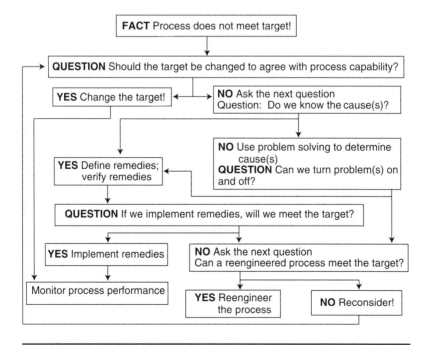

Figure 5.10   Problem solving or reengineering.

addressed first, the organization can often avoid an expensive and more risky "clean sheet of paper" approach.

Reengineering

Sometimes we find that there are very few problems with the current process and its activities. Indeed, the process may be performing as well as possible given the technology and basic process flow that is in place. In this case, we may decide to reengineer the process using completely different process flows and perhaps more advanced technology.

Considerations to keep in mind include:

- Gain a clear understanding of the reengineering project objectives.
  - –Define measures and targets.
  - –Determine how you will know when the project is successfully completed.
- Manage all reengineering efforts as projects with formal project plans.
- Set up a dedicated (not part-time) project team.
- Develop a complete definition of the new technology to be adopted.
- Determine if the current workers who perform the old process are the appropriate people to perform the new one.
  - –Capability to make the change.
  - –What to do with the excess people or where to get more or different people.
  - –Training requirements.
- Use process mapping.
- Consider what can go wrong and do failure modes and effects analysis (FMEA).
- Determine steps for transition to the reengineered process.
- Consider actions needed to optimize the new process.

Many sources of information provide greater detail on reengineering.[8]

DETERMINE AND MEASURE KEY INDEPENDENT PROCESS VARIABLES

For many processes, particularly those that are more capital-intensive, it may be critical to understand which process parameters are the causes of process performance. This concept is important in solving the basic problems that cause processes to miss targets. It is also important in developing new or reengineered processes because it helps establish which process parameters should be monitored or measured over time to ensure that the process continues to meet requirements. The concept, which is quite simple, was mentioned in Chapter 4 (Figure 4.5 shows the example related to the sweet taste of candy). While the concept is more complex than this simplistic example, its power is often ignored.

The idea is that most process output measures cannot be directly changed. Rather, they are "response" variables. That is, they respond to changes in other variables within the process. These other variables can be changed and are called "independent" variables. To get better results out of the process, we must determine which of the many independent variables in the process affect process performance and learn to optimize them. The most important concept is the opposite of this. It is critical to remember that the *process output results (response variables) are very difficult to change unless we identify and change the independent variables.* We cannot make the candy sweeter unless we determine what makes it sweet and change the amount of the ingredients that make it sweet! Likewise, it is not possible to change the output rate of a chemical process directly. Instead we must change things like input flow rate, heat input, and the like. Lest you think this concept applies only to capital-intensive processes like automated machining or chemical plants, let's look at a very simple example: the little boy with his radio-controlled car, illustrated in Figure 5.11. We see that the

Figure 5.11   Simple example of response and independent variables.

actual independent variable is skill as determined by the amount of practice by the boy.

For critical activities that must be completed correctly by employees to achieve a desired result, it may be that the real controlling independent variables are the effectiveness of training and amount of practice.

You may be wondering how to determine which of the many variables of your process are the ones that, when changed, will provide better outputs. One way to determine this is to ask those working in the process. Often, they know (or at least have a good idea) which things these *might* be. It is useful to have the workgroup or process team develop an Ishikawa fishbone diagram to work out the likely candidates. Figure 5.12 illustrates one such diagram for a chemical process. The methodology would be similar for a new or reengineered process.

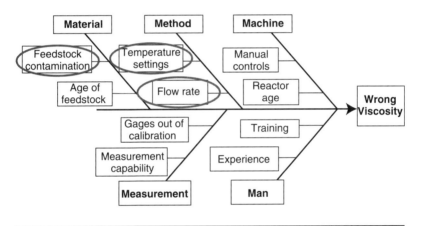

Figure 5.12   Fishbone diagrams can help determine independent process variables.

In this case the issue was the variability in viscosity of the output product. The process also had insufficient process output to meet peak customer demand. It seemed that each time the customer wanted to buy more product, the viscosity would go out of specs. The pet theory of the operators was that when flow rate went up, quality went down. The process engineers had always thought that the real culprit was the feedstock that contained a trace chemical that was considered a contaminant and affected viscosity. They complained that management had always refused to use feedstock with lower contamination levels because it cost more. When the process team developed the fishbone, it was easy to guess that both these groups might be correct. Figure 5.13 shows that it was decided to run some simple experiments at higher flow rate using both the normal feedstock and some feedstock of better purity.

It was also decided to vary the reaction temperature. The results, as shown on the scatter diagrams in Figures 5.14 and 5.15, were astonishing. Changing the reaction temperature had no significant effect, but varying the flow rate and the feedstock purity showed spectacular results. Figure 5.14

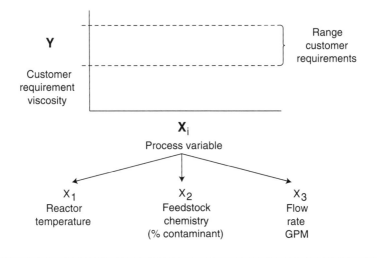

Figure 5.13   Possible independent variables controlling viscosity.

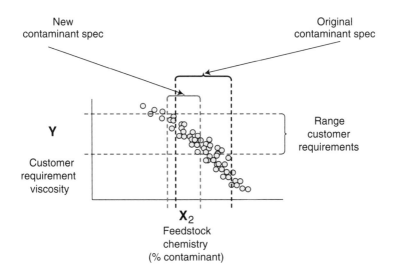

Figure 5.14   Tighter tolerances on feedstock contaminant give better viscosity.

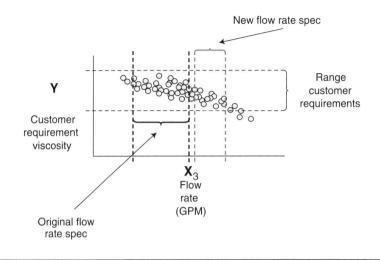

Figure 5.15   Higher flow rate showed no degradation in viscosity.

shows that with tightened contamination specifications on the feedstock, there was a marked improvement in the ability to control viscosity. This came with a cost penalty, but the organization was able to guarantee shipping the right viscosity.

And that is not all. The biggest sales issue had been lack of capacity during peak demand periods. Figure 5.15 illustrates that the organization was able to increase flow rate significantly while still maintaining the viscosity required. The ability to produce additional product more than compensated for the low-contaminant feedstock costs. Since the people who ran the process were well aligned with the objective of meeting all customer needs, this process management study was a great success. And these operators were committed to holding the gains. But nothing was left to chance. The process specifications were changed to reflect the new flow rate, and procurement specifications were modified to lower the permissible contaminant level. These actions ensured that the changes are subject to internal audit, further reducing the probability that the gains will be lost over time.

A fishbone diagram and simple scatter plots were used to analyze process performance. More sophisticated approaches may be required for more complex analyses. For the more complicated analyses, it may be advisable to employ statistical analysis tools such as design of experiments methodology to determine the optimal combination of variables impacting process output.[9]

PREVENTIVE ACTION

It would be ideal if our processes never had failures, upsets, or problems. Have you ever considered how much it would cost for you to include in your processes sufficient preventive measures so that nothing would go wrong ever? With conventional thinking it certainly would cost a lot, but the cost of major process upsets or failures can be great also. What is needed is a change in thinking. *The best time to prevent problems is when processes are being developed or changed.* That is when preventive action can be done easiest, and if we are smart about it, these actions can actually reduce costs. Let's look at three opportunities available to us.

Create Simplicity If You Can

It would be good if every process could be simple enough that linear relationships could be established between independent and response variables. For such simple relationships, the process can be controlled with well-known statistical tools, as we described in our chemical process example. It would also be great if the interactions between independent variables were simple enough that they could always be studied using simple design of experiments techniques. It would be great if the interactions among the various steps in every process were few and simple. Unfortunately, for many processes, this is not reality. It is common for a process to have extremely complex interactions among its independent variables. The section in Chapter 7 on Preventive Action—Chaos, Complexity and Simple Solutions describes why complex processes may behave in a chaotic manner.

For some complex processes it is feasible to describe the relationships with a set of partial differential equations and to control the process with computers. If the process is complex enough, even this may not be practical.

Even if computer control is feasible, most of the time, for complex processes the real answer is to *simplify*. Even when computers are used, simpler is almost always better. Process simplification is important not only because it can save money, but also because it prevents chaotic process behavior that becomes apparent only after the process has been operating for a while. *Simplification is probably the best of all preventive actions.*

Process Failure Modes and Effects Analysis (PFMEA)

PFMEA gives us a method for managing the risks associated with potential process failures. PFMEA is a technique for studying the causes and effects of failures before they occur. In addition to analysis of the potential failure modes and their effects, it is very common to analyze the criticality of each potential failure mode. It is best to use this technique during process development or when major process improvements or changes are being planned.

PFMEA starts with the process flowchart. Each activity is reviewed and potential failures are listed in an FMEA table and analyzed:

- For each potential failure, the possible failure modes are listed.

- For each failure mode, the effect that such a failure could have is described.

- For each potential failure, an estimate (on a scale of 1 to 10 with 10 being worst) is made of severity, probability (or frequency) of occurrence, and detectability (ability to detect the potential cause and prevent the failure).

- The rankings are multiplied to give a risk priority number that can be used to prioritize preventive actions.

An evaluation is made of the potential failure modes, and actions are considered to prevent occurrence or minimize the impact of potential failures with highest priority.

Care must be taken to control the scope of the PFMEA, while retaining its integrity. Also, information from a PFMEA can often be useful to other activities in an organization. PFMEA outputs should be shared with organizations performing related duties. PFMEA results should be shared with organizations that will operate and maintain the processes.[10]

Plan for Uncertainties

Some processes contain activities or steps that involve a great deal of uncertainty. For example, the process for managing the maintenance process will necessarily have a step in which the availability of a critical repair part is determined. No matter how well we have selected the parts to be on hand, it is reasonable for the maintenance process team to consider including in the process a provision for the situation where a critical part is not available. In other words, think through a "plan B" for key foreseeable uncertainties in the process.

Chapter 7 will deal more completely with the topic of preventive action.

IMPLEMENTATION OF PROCESS CHANGES

There can be no improvement without change, and change never happens without implementation. It does little good and is a waste of time to prepare process maps, analyze data, determine causes, and develop new process flows if we do not implement change. Often, organizations leave implementation to chance and do little planning for it. Sometimes leaders do not even recognize that process improvement involves change management. This is unfortunate, because well-planned implementation is needed for change to be effective. The process team should start planning for implementation as soon as they have an understanding of the nature of the changes to be made. There should be an informal implementation plan for even minor changes and quick fixes. Plans for implementing large changes (such as major process changes or reengineering projects) need to be formal, well thought out, and tested. Implementing a complete process reengineering of an entire business requires more thought than a single major process change, but the considerations are similar. In all cases, it is necessary to communicate the change to all involved people and to gain their support. Some issues to consider in planning include:

- Developing implementation sequences and milestones so that things get done in the correct order and within a defined timeframe.

- Understanding the behaviors of personnel in the current process and what changes will be needed in behavior for the new or changed process.

- Hiring of any new personnel who will be needed.

- Determining training, skills, or education required.

- Listing the potential barriers that may be faced in making the change and planning actions to avoid them.

- Planning communications in terms of content and timing.

- Planning for the impact the changes will have on processes and people not directly involved in the project.

- Understanding potential hidden costs associated with the change such as learning curve issues.

In addition to planning the implementation, consideration should be given to how the process or process changes can be tested. Testing is needed to validate process designs and to verify that the new or revised process will meet objectives when implementation is completed. Pilot or small-scale implementations may be possible. Modeling and process design reviews may also be part of the verification process.

Brien Palmer in *Making Change Work: Practical Tools for Overcoming Human Resistance to Change* describes seven steps that should be taken to provide reasonable assurance that a major change will be successful. Palmer writes:

. . . all changes move from the current state, through a transition phase, into the desired improvement state. In the beginning, it is important to create, or affirm, a broadly understood need for the change (Creating a shared need), along with an idea of what the outcome will look like (Shaping a vision). As the change effort gets underway, and throughout until the end, it must always have a sufficient amount of resources dedicated to it (Mobilizing commitment). As work gets completed, you must have a way to track it (Monitoring progress) and assure that it reaches completion (Finishing the job).[11]

MEASURES OF PROCESS PERFORMANCE

As we discussed earlier in this chapter there are two basic types of process measures. We can measure independent variables and response variables. Both types are needed. Managers tend to want to monitor overall process performance, and that is best done by measuring the process outputs—the process's response variables. Since process control and improvement may not be achievable by measuring the response variables alone, it is necessary to measure data on the key independent variables. One common approach is to monitor the output data while maintaining the data on key independent variables to analyze any process performance issues. A better approach is to find the set of independent variables that control performance. Careful selection of measures and proper collection of data provide a basis for continual process improvement. These measures of process performance are included in the organization's scorecard, discussed in Chapter 4.

THE ROLE OF TOP MANAGEMENT

It is important for top managers to be involved in process management activities. Top managers' roles include determination of the projects to be undertaken, providing resources, and periodically reviewing results. They should be familiar with the measures being used for each project and able to determine if the project is on track.

Top managers' actions can make or break a project. If a top executive shows interest for one project but has no interest in a second project that has similar magnitude and improvement opportunity, it is common for the second project to fail. It may be that the second project appears to the executive to be ill advised and to have little chance to achieve its targets. In such cases, the executive needs to take the time to determine the true value potential of the project. If the project's potential return is inadequate, the executive needs to face up to that fact by canceling the project and redirecting the resources. This responsibility brings us to another job of top managers: constant vigilance. Vigilance is needed to detect and act on signs that resources need to be reallocated.

Constant vigilance is also needed to ensure the overall system remains relevant under changing conditions. This broader issue is covered in Chapter 10.

WHAT CAN I DO NOW?

We can ask several questions:

- How does your organization make money and satisfy customer requirements?

- Which processes have interfaces with your organization's customers?

- What are the processes to satisfy customer requirements and add value?

- Have you used process mapping and value stream analysis to understand and improve your processes?

- Do you use systems thinking to understand the behavior of your management system?

- Do you think about preventing future problems when you develop or improve processes?

From the answers to these questions, it may be productive to distill out the processes that appear to be the keys to satisfying customers and making money and to be sure we understand how they work.

You may not yet know the true key measures of performance, but the processes you identify should align with the list of key drivers you developed when you read Chapter 4.

Consideration of such issues will reinforce the basic concept of process management—to measure, manage, and improve the key processes and their interrelationships so that key drivers of performance are enhanced and overall business performance is improved.

6

Embrace Continual Improvement

". . . could you and I not with Him conspire
To grasp this sorry scheme of things entire,
Would we not shatter it to bits—and then
Remold it nearer to the heart's desire."

"Rubáiyát" of Omar Khayyam

In Chapter 5 we discussed the concepts and tools of process management and stated that it is one of the best ways to focus on meeting quality and business objectives. The concept of continual improvement involves making processes and results better over time. This chapter focuses on improving processes. We will discuss system level improvement in Chapter 10.

ISO 9001 requires continual improvement of the effectiveness of the quality management system and describes a loop of improvement that flows through the standard. The requirements start in clauses 5.4.2 and 8.1 with the requirement that the system be planned in such a way that its processes are continually improved.

The cycle of improvement starts in clause 5.3 with a requirement for a commitment to continual improvement of the QMS in the quality policy. Clause 5.4.1 requires that objectives be set with this commitment to improvement in mind. Clause 8.2 requires that the organization monitor and measure products, processes, customer satisfaction, and audit results. Clause 8.4 requires that data be identified, collected, and analyzed to determine opportunities for improvement. Clauses 8.5.2 and 8.5.3, on corrective action and preventive action, require that action be taken to address the causes of problems and potential problems. Clause 5.6 requires that top management identify opportunities for improvement as an output of management review.

The cycle starts with top management setting policy and ends with management review, where top managers not only identify additional opportuni-

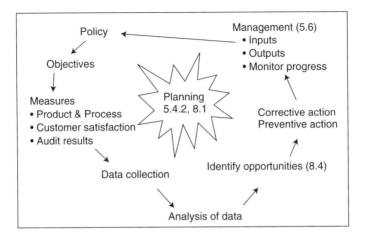

Figure 6.1 ISO 9001 requirements for planned continual improvement.

ties but also review the policy and objectives to make certain they remain relevant. Figure 6.1 illustrates the relationships between these concepts.

To meet the minimal requirements of ISO 9001, an organization needs to have thought through, planned, and implemented its processes for improvement. But ISO 9001, even when we refer to the definition in ISO 9000, does not provide us with a complete understanding of continual improvement. ISO 9000:2000 defines continual improvement, as shown in Table 6.1. It is interesting that the note under the definition describes some of the improvement requirements of ISO 9001 but not all. For example, the quality policy and top management focus that is present in ISO 9001 is missing in the definition.

The basic requirement of ISO 9001 may appear to be somewhat narrow because it only addresses "effectiveness of the quality management system" and that narrow wording is intentional. For example, ISO 9001 does not intend to require improvement of process efficiency.

Table 6.1 ISO 9000 definition of continual improvement.

Continual improvement—recurring activity to increase the ability to fulfill requirements (3.1.2)

NOTE: The process (3.4.1) of establishing objectives and finding opportunities for improvement is a continual process through the use of audit findings (3.9.5) and audit conclusions (3.9.6), analysis of data, management reviews (3.8.7) or other means and generally leads to corrective action (3.6.5) or preventive action (3.6.4).

Source: ANSI/ISO/ASQ Q9000–2000.

Table 6.2 Principles related to continual improvement.

ISO 9000 principle: continual improvement of the organization's overall performance should be a permanent objective of the organization.
Principle from Chapter 1: continual improvement, innovation and learning— organizations achieve excellence by continually learning, innovating and improving.
Source of ISO 9000 principle: ANSI/ISO/ASQ Q9000–2000.

For the organization focused on continual improvement, a broader understanding of continual improvement is necessary. With the definition in ISO 9000, improvement depends upon the requirements. If there is a requirement for a better or less expensive product, then the continual improvement concept might be applied. If there is a requirement for improvement of the organization's overall performance, then continual improvement of performance would be an organizational objective. In Chapter 1 we discussed the principles of continual improvement. Table 6.2 gives both the ISO 9000 principle on continual improvement and the principle of organizational management.

Note that the ISO 9000 principle says that all organizations should have a permanent objective of performance improvement. The organizational management principle from Chapter 1 indicates that continual improvement is related to innovation and learning. Achieving excellence requires all three!

By now we should be convinced that improvement is important, but what is *continual* improvement?

THE BASICS OF CONTINUAL IMPROVEMENT

Annex B to ISO 9004:2000 can help us to better understand the basics of continual improvement. It discusses two very different types of continual improvement: incremental improvement and breakthrough.[1] ISO 9004 describes these concepts, as shown in Table 6.3.

There are several ideas given:

1. Continual improvement can be either incremental or breakthrough in nature.

2. Continual improvement always implies process improvement.

3. Improvement happens project-by-project. J. M. Juran used to say, "All improvement occurs project-by-project and in no other way."

4. Involvement of people and teamwork are prerequisites to continual improvement.

Table 6.3   ISO 9004:2000 Annex B description of continual improvement.

There are two fundamental ways to conduct continual process improvement, as follows:

a) breakthrough projects which either lead to revision and improvement of existing processes or the implementation of new processes; these are usually carried out by cross-functional teams outside routine operations

b) small-step ongoing improvement activities conducted within existing processes by people working in those processes.

Breakthrough projects usually involve significant redesign of existing processes and should include:

— definition of the objectives and an outline of the improvement project

— analysis of the existing process (the "as-is" process) and realizing opportunities for change

— definition and planning of improvement to the process

— implementation of the improvement

— verification and validation of the process improvement

— evaluation of the improvement achieved, including lessons learned

Breakthrough projects should be conducted in an effective and efficient way using project management methods. After completion of the change, a new project plan should be the basis for continuing process management.

People in the organization are the best sources of ideas for small-step or ongoing process improvement and often participate in projects as work groups. Small-step ongoing process improvement activities should be controlled in order to understand their effect. The people in the organization that are involved should be provided with the authority, technical support and necessary resources for the changes associated with the improvement.

Source: ANSI/ISO/ASQ Q9004–2000.

There is one aspect of continual improvement that is not explicitly addressed in ISO 9004:2000—that it is important to look for those situations that have been "forever" problem areas for the organization. These are the chronic problems that have existed and been accepted as a way of life. Even though these chronic problem areas may be known, they can become institutionalized. Significant gains in efficiency and effectiveness can result from questioning why we should tolerate such situations. For example, we should question a process in which we have embedded rework to correct nonconformities in 10 percent of the items produced. A fresh look at such issues with a view to improvement can produce spectacular gains.

Now let's look at improvement, starting with the notions of incremental and breakthrough improvement.

CONTINUAL IMPROVEMENT—INCREMENTAL AND BREAKTHROUGH

Let's review these two concepts by looking at an example. We will assume that a process has been established to achieve a key output in our organization. We have a focus on continual improvement and our objectives are such that we expect small annual improvements in performance. Figure 6.2 shows the performance of the process. We establish incremental improvement as an objective of the team that operates the process. We can see in Figure 6.2 that over the first five years of operations, the team has made substantial progress. While there have been some setbacks, their incremental improvements have yielded significant overall improvement. No single improvement was great, but the long-term effects of small improvement projects over these first five years have been quite positive. No project has been very expensive. In fact, we gave the team no additional resources and absorbed all of the improvement costs in the operating budget. These were the best of times!

Sometime in the fifth year one of the engineers working on the process read an article in a trade journal. A competitor described how they operate a similar process and gave some data that piqued the engineer's interest. The data indicated in an obscure way that the competitor's process performs better than ours. As a result of the article, we decided to look at the performance of this process against similar processes operated by other organizations. We

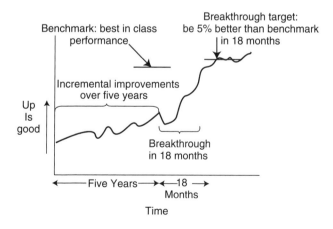

Figure 6.2   Continual improvement—incremental and breakthrough.

were unable to visit a competitor but we did a benchmarking study with several other noncompetitive organizations that use a similar process. We found that the best performing processes are about twice as good as ours. We also discover process differences that enable the other organizations to be able to exceed our performance levels—sometimes by very wide margins.

Since this is a key process for our organization, we set a target to make major changes in performance quickly (about 18 months in our example, shown in Figure 6.2). This means that dramatic changes will be required. In most cases, these changes will involve capital expenditures. They will also have much higher risk than any of the incremental improvements made over the past several years. A project team is put together. The team is led by a key manager and supported by engineers and others important to success. Approval is obtained for the capital expenditures needed to improve the technology of the equipment involved. Training is provided for the operations team to use the new process. An implementation plan is developed to ensure startup success. The implementation plan provides for continued operation of the old process as the new reengineered process is developed and implemented. We are successful. Over the targeted 18 months, we exceed our goals. We indeed made a breakthrough.

Notice that breakthrough improvements are very different in nature from incremental improvements. We expect incremental improvements from the people operating the process, while breakthrough requires outside resources. It is typical for breakthrough projects to cost more and to have more risk of failing to meet targets than projects to achieve incremental improvements.

Table 6.4 compares these and other characteristics of incremental and breakthrough improvements. This has great implications for how we man-

Table 6.4 Differences between incremental and breakthrough improvements.

Characteristics	Tendency	
	Incremental	**Breakthrough**
People involved	People working in the process	Managers, engineers, consultants
Size of changes	Small incremental changes	Big changes
Types of changes	Practices, procedures, simplification, process fool-proofing	Technology, new equipment, major process changes
Results	Small improvements	Large "jumps" in performance
Cost of projects	Low, generally included in operating budget	High, may involve capital investment

age projects. *If you expect small improvements, don't invest a lot of capital! If you expect breakthrough in performance, don't expect to get by on the cheap* by demanding that the people who work in the process make major improvements.

IMPROVE THE PROCESSES

In Chapter 5 we discussed the notion that all work is best accomplished when we manage activities to create an outcome together with resources and controls. In short, all work involves a process to transform inputs to outputs. If this is true, it must also be true that the way to improve anything is to improve either the process that creates it or the inputs, resources, or controls for that process!

The process management tools covered in Chapter 5 are important to both incremental and breakthrough improvements. This means that almost everyone in the organization needs to have a basic understanding of process concepts as shown in Figure 5.3.

The basic ideas related to the SIPOC model shown in Figure 5.4 also needs to be clear to everyone and they need to have sufficient knowledge to perform valid process analysis. Providing this understanding implies training, of course. But it also implies practice. Training everyone in these ideas and the related tools is wasted if they don't get a chance to successfully employ them. It is important to practice finding the proper independent variables that affect process output.

CONTINUAL IMPROVEMENT—COMMON CAUSES AND SPECIAL CAUSES

Often, continual improvement requires eliminating the real causes of problems. To the purist, there are two basic types of causes. To the pragmatist, there are three:

- Special causes, which are not part of the planned process

- Common causes, which are inherent in the process

- Phantom causes, which are situations or conditions that appear to be causes and are often "corrected" but actually have no effect on the process

Perhaps phantom causes are the most common. How often have you seen your organization brainstorm a list of causes for a problem and select the easiest two or three items to implement? Organizations do this all the time. And the interesting thing about phantom causes is that often the problem mysteriously "disappears" when they are "corrected." When this happens, the organization celebrates success when it has actually just seen a natural variation in a process that has embedded common causes that remain unknown.

In one organization, a process was observed that was treated this way. Control charts were kept for the process and action was taken every time the process went "out of control." Usually, the action resulted in an apparent improvement in performance. In fact, some of these were celebrated as great successes.

When the organization was asked to prepare a long-term chart of the process results, it became apparent that over 15 years the process had been stable and in control at an average of 15 percent defective. Some of the declines in performance had been introduced by sudden changes in production volume, changes in raw materials, and other real "special" causes that had to be addressed and solved. But the majority of the causes that had been addressed over the years were actually phantom causes.

The real issue was that the process was not inherently capable of better than 15 percent average performance. The cause of this lack of process capability was known to the engineers responsible for process engineering. The production executives remained unconvinced until they saw the costs associated with the 15 percent defective process over the 15-year period shown on the graph. They then became energized and demanded a solution from the process engineers. Because the engineers knew what to do, it became a matter of implementation. With convinced production executives, it was only a matter of time—but not much time. Over a six-month period the defect percentage was driven permanently down to 5 percent. Over the next three years it was further reduced to less than 1 percent. The trick was in *implementation* of known changes to address common causes of defects.

Organizations should recognize the difference between these types of causes so that they do not think they have made a long-term process improvement when they have only addressed a special cause or a phantom cause.

CONTINUAL IMPROVEMENT—PROJECT BY PROJECT

Improvements are much more likely to be achieved if they are planned, if targets and completion dates are established, and if responsibilities are defined. Whether it is a small project in the customer service group or a big project involving capital equipment, we should manage improvement project by project. The definition of a project given in ISO 9000:2000 is shown in Table 6.5.

Table 6.5   Definition of "project."

Project—unique process (3.4.1), consisting of a set of coordinated and controlled activities with start and finish dates, undertaken to achieve an objective conforming to specific requirements (3.1.2), including the constraints of time, cost and resources

Note 1: An individual project can form part of a larger project structure.
Note 2: In some projects the objectives are refined and the product characteristics (3.5.1) defined
          progressively as the project proceeds.
Note 3: The outcome of a project may be one or several units of product (3.4.2).
Note 4: Adapted from ISO 10006:1997.

Source: ANSI/ISO/ASQ Q9000–2000.

A major characteristic of a project is the concept of control. We set targets and control our activities so that we meet them on a defined timeline with defined resources. Using project management techniques implies:

- Having a defined and measurable objective, documented in a requirements specification

- Having a project plan and keeping it up to date—the plan includes who will do what and by when

- Determining who the project team members should be—include any outside help that is needed

- Determining the resources that will be needed

- Determining what the project will cost

With a clearly defined objective, a plan for achieving the objective, adequate resources (human and capital), and mechanisms for measuring and monitoring performance, every project, large or small, can be successful. For small projects, management can be accomplished with little overhead and bureaucracy—perhaps by conducting periodic project review meetings. For larger projects, project management software may be appropriate. But large or small, every successful improvement project contributes to the success of the organization.

CONTINUAL IMPROVEMENT—TEAMWORK IS ALWAYS BEST

Teamwork is necessary for the improvement of all processes except those completely controlled by one individual. It is often said that teamwork is important because several heads are better than one. This may or may not be true in any given situation. We have all been through teamwork games that demonstrate the value of using the ideas of several people over using only our own. Of course, there are many cases where this concept fails in practice. For example, in the case of complex technology, the worker using the equipment may not even understand it, much less be able to make significant improvements in its performance. The engineer who designed the equipment may know what changes will improve its performance. The worker knows day-to-day problems and the engineer knows what to do for improvement. They need to work together. It is not just because more people can come to the right solution to problems that we need teamwork. Another reason is in implementation! We need teamwork and involvement of everyone because we need everyone's buy-in to make changes needed for improvement. *The engineer's best change is worthless if the worker won't, or can't, run the process that way.*

LEAN, SIX SIGMA, KAIZEN, JIT, COQ, AND THE REST

Many organizations become engaged in major programs initiated to facilitate improvement. They come with many names such as:

- **Lean manufacturing/Kaizen/JIT**—waste elimination

- **Six Sigma**—reduction in variation and improvement of quality

- **COQ**—reducing the cost of quality

Programs like these should be integrated into the organization's management system and can be quite useful in driving continual improvement. Many organizations use combinations of them and others as well. Resist the temptation to treat any of these as a program separate from the overall management system. Rather, we recommend that you find ways to integrate your efforts to avoid wasted time, energy, and cost.

CONTINUAL IMPROVEMENT— IMPLEMENTATION

The technical details of project management are needed for success, but full support of all key managers is critical. Well-known solutions often go unimplemented because there was insufficient buy-in across the organization. In a column on quality management in *Quality Digest,* Dr. A. Blanton Godfrey commented:

Time after time in consulting projects, I've seen the same thing happen. Analysis leads to a clear solution, but the solution is never implemented. Something in the company culture prevents people from facing or perhaps using, the facts. Instead, we continue doing things the way we always have . . . the organizations should have created steering teams with representatives from every site. They should have agreed on the improvement plan.[2]

Outstanding leadership is required to get this kind of involvement and agreement. Managers need to recognize chronic problems and drive the development and implementation of solutions. While quality professionals need to be good at facilitating continual improvement, it is far more important for the top managers to be active in the improvement effort.

WHAT CAN I DO NOW?

Take an inventory of formal processes in place (for example, those described in a procedure) that require consideration of continual improvement.

- Are you considering both incremental and breakthrough improvement?

- Is management review effective in initiating projects that will result in improvement?

- Are your improvement projects fact-based, that is, based on analysis of performance data?

If the organization has not formalized and institutionalized continual improvement, what can be done to move in that direction?

If your organization has formalized and institutionalized continual improvement, what can be done to improve the improvement processes?

7

Change Your Thinking on Corrective Action and Preventive Action

"It's a bad plan that can't be changed."

Pubilius Syrus
Maxims

In Chapter 3 we mentioned that corrective action and preventive action were among the most powerful concepts that can be used by an organization to encourage improvement. But like any tools, they must be used properly to obtain optimal results. Indeed, a power saw can cut a lot of lumber, but if not used properly, it can also cut off one's finger.

One of the most common issues in effecting improvement in organizations is confusing correction and corrective action. Let's start by considering the definitions in Table 7.1 and Table 7.2.

Table 7.1   Definition of "correction."

Correction—an action to eliminate a detected nonconformity

Source: ANSI/ISO/ASQ Q 9000-2000

Table 7.2 Definition of "corrective action."

Corrective action—an action to eliminate the cause of a detected nonconformity or other undesirable situation

Source: ANSI/ISO/ASQ Q9000-2000

And while we are considering definitions, preventive action is defined in Table 7.3.

Table 7.3 Definition of "preventive action."

Preventive action—action to eliminate the cause of a potential nonconformity or otherwise undesirable situation

Source ANSI/ISO/ASQ Q9000-2000

CORRECTION AND CORRECTIVE ACTION

Usage of these concepts is as much a matter of ensuring understanding and making expectations clear as it is of adhering to specific definitions. If management ensures that everyone understands what the terms mean and makes expectations clear, the focus can be on taking the right action to correct or prevent a problem or undesirable situation.

Table 7.4 provides an overview of typical correction, corrective action and preventive action issues, examples of actions that may be taken to address the issues and examples of typical tools that could be used.

Let's consider correction and corrective action first. Notice the difference in the definitions. There are more words in the definition of corrective action. This must mean that corrective action is different from correction.

Table 7.4 Types of action.

Type of action	Type of issue	Examples of actions to take	Typical Tools
Correction	Undesirable situation or nonconformity	Correct the specific nonconformity, e.g., scrap, repair	Process for determining disposition
Corrective action		Determine and correct the cause of the existing undesirable situation or nonconformity	Problem-solving tools
Preventive action	Potential problem or potential nonconformity	Define, prioritize and prevent important potential problems or nonconformities	FMEA, risk analysis, prioritization, availability analysis, fault-tree analysis

And indeed it is. *It is an unfortunate reality that correction is often confused with, or substituted for, corrective action.* Many believe that eliminating a nonconformity (for example, by rework or repair) is corrective action. It is not, and thinking that it is represents an incomplete understanding of the corrective action concept.

To illustrate the failure to grasp the difference between correction and corrective action, consider the examples shown in Tables 7.5 and 7.6, the contents of which were excerpted from actual corrective action forms in real organizations.

In these simplistic examples the "corrective actions" did not eliminate the *cause* of the nonconformities, although they did indeed eliminate the nonconformities.

Organizations all too often correct nonconformity or undesirable situations but do not take the next steps to consider elimination of the cause of the nonconformity or undesirable situation. But the problem with understanding the corrective action concept does not stop here. Organizations also tend to think of certain actions they take after product disasters to recover customers and good will as corrective actions. Withdrawing the product from the marketplace or recalling and replacing products may address the good will issue, but *unless the cause of the problem is corrected, the organization has not taken corrective action.*

Organizations often take containment actions by sorting nonconforming product for processes when correcting the causes would be expensive, perhaps even requiring the purchase of new technology. While such con-

---

Table 7.5   Ineffective corrective action in manufacturing.

Corrective action request form
Issue: Manufactured part does not meet requirement
Diagnosis: Operator error
Corrective Action: Rework the part
Signed: <u>Manufacturing manager</u>   Approved: <u>Quality Manager</u>

Table 7.6   Ineffective corrective action in service.

Corrective action request form
Issue: Guest complained that there are no clean towels in room 105
Diagnosis: Cleaning staff forgot to put clean towels in room during daily service
Corrective Action: Send clean towels to the room and remind cleaning staff to put clean towels in every room
Signed: <u>Cleaning staff manager</u>   Approved: <u>Quality Manager</u>

tainment strategies may be appropriate business decisions (if made consciously), they are not corrective action because they do not address the causes of the nonconformities.

It is not uncommon for organizations to address only symptomatic causes of nonconformity and other problems. If there is a process that produces defects, the organization may find it easy to add a second process to correct those defects or identify them by sorting. If a service process delivers nonconforming service, the organization can add customer support personnel to mollify customers. These actions are not necessarily bad as short-term correction measures, but they are bad if they become permanent. Addressing only symptoms often results in the institutionalization of extra activities needed because the initial value-adding activities are not capable of meeting requirements. Sometimes these extra operations (extra people, extra inspections, and so on) linger even longer than the life of the product by becoming inherent in new or updated product or service processes. This is unfortunate. Organizations need to recognize these actions as being short-term containment activities and move to quickly address the actual causes. Addressing symptoms tends to restrict the organization's ability to find root causes. It tends to turn off the signals. We apply the symptomatic solution over and over sometimes because we don't see the signals of the real underlying issues. *So, the organization must stop calling correction of symptomatic causes "corrective action."* It is much more desirable to use some other term like "symptom correction" or "containment."

This does not mean that there must be a formal corrective action project to eliminate the cause of every detected nonconformity. Sometimes it is justified to pursue corrective action; sometimes it may not be. Such decisions are management decisions that depend on many factors such as likelihood of reoccurrence, cost of a fix, and impact on customer perceptions.

When faced with nonconformity, the organization should make a conscious decision regarding the need to pursue corrective action. Answer the question: "Do we need to find and eliminate the causes of the nonconformity?"

So how do we know when to just correct, contain, or recover and when to pursue corrective action? And if we do want to "eliminate causes of nonconformity," how do we do it?

One of the most profitable investments an organization can make is in the education of every individual in the organization in the art and science of performing true corrective action every day when encountering "nonconformity" or "other undesirable situations." The reason for this is simple. We live in an imperfect world. Machines malfunction. Random variation occurs. Humans behave humanly (if not humanely). Hence, nonconformity and undesirable states or situations are going to be a part of our existence—and on a regular basis. Although "error free performance" and "zero defects" are our goal, thousands of years of civilization have provided ample evidence that, in reality, we should expect nonconformity and other undesirable situations to be a regular part of our daily existence.

We are not suggesting that a vibrant corrective action process will eliminate all nonconformity. We are suggesting that organizations need to embrace the notion of true corrective action. We need to change the attitudes that perpetuate ineffective action to attitudes that result in real corrective action on the problems important to success. Table 7.7 illustrates examples of what we believe are appropriate changes in thinking. Top managers need to think of corrective action as a process that must be encouraged—even if it takes a little longer to implement corrective action than making "the quick fix."

Table 7.7 Changes in thinking.

Attitudes	
Old thinking	**New thinking**
• Corrective action request (CAR) forms	• Problem-solving projects
• Fast action	• Analysis and study
• Symptoms	• Root cause analysis
• Decisions by managers	• Problem-solving teams
• Counts of open and closed CARs	• Measurable results

CORRECTIVE ACTION PROCESS

Top management cannot "speak out of both sides of the mouth" on this issue. The people in the organization know whether their leaders want real corrective action or the quick fix. Corrective action is not easy. It takes time and effort and may require involvement of several areas of the organization to implement an effective process.

Figure 7.1 describes a typical approach to comprehensive corrective action in the form of a flow diagram.

The reason so many steps are shown in Figure 7.1 is that effective corrective action needs to be a systematic journey from identification of a problem to its ultimate resolution. It is encouraging to know that for each step in a corrective action journey, there are tools available to enhance our ability to perform each of the activities.

The corrective action process is further complicated by the fact that requests for corrective action can arise from almost any corner or process in the organization.

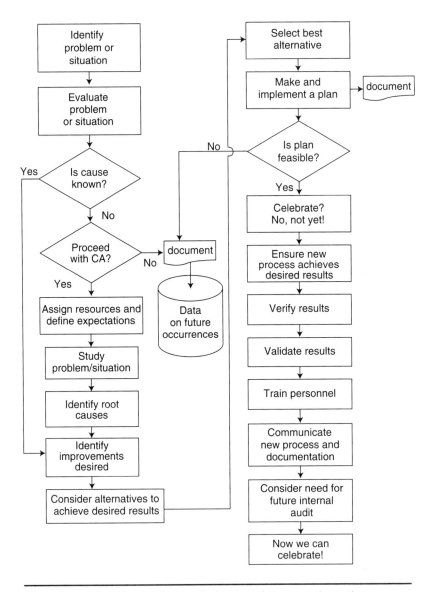

Figure 7.1 Flow diagram for a typical approach to corrective action.

The need for corrective action, for example, could arise as a result of:

- Customer complaints
  - –Product/service quality
  - –Product/service reliability
  - –Literature
  - –Billing accuracy
  - –Delivery timing
- Inefficiencies in processes related to:
  - –Materials
  - –Methods
  - –People
  - –Equipment
  - –Measurement
- Lack of adequate processes or criteria of acceptability

- Lack of process capability

- Human error

- Lack of information

- Lack of adequate resources (tools, equipment, and other resources)

Often it can be more valuable to correct causes of problems in support processes than those directly related to products and services.

CORRECTIVE ACTION TOOLS AND TRAINING

We mentioned earlier that an organization requires investment to achieve a culture of dedication to corrective action. To be effective, the capability must exist for the right individual to use the right tool to perform a particular task. One can consider an analogy to building a house (or a cathedral). Perhaps a house could be completed by one individual using an ax, a hammer, a wrench, and a saw—but the project would take time and the results would be crude compared to a house built by a crew of specialists (plumbers, roofers, electricians, carpenters) using tools such as power nailers, compound miter saws, and compressors.

Powerful tools in the hands of skilled practitioners will yield excellent results quickly and with minimum use of resources.

But the best high-tech tools are not all that is needed. We must have the right tools. The best carpenter will be ineffective in wiring a three-way light fixture with laser-guided miter saw technology. So it is in an organization. We need the proper tools and staff, and we need to train our people to use the tools to get good results. We cannot give an electrician a pipe wrench to wire a house and expect a good result. Likewise, we should not ask customer support center personnel to analyze call data without providing training in Pareto analysis, making check sheets, or computing averages.

If an organization wants to reap the benefits that can be gained from changing the organization's thinking on how to address corrective action, it needs to invest in training its staff on the tools that can be used.

The tools that can be used to achieve corrective action are many—hundreds, perhaps thousands. And many books have been written about the appropriate tools and how they should be used.[1] For every block in the flow diagram in Figure 7.1, there are tools and techniques that could be used.

We should always remember that the tools are best implemented within the quality management system, not implemented separately. The tools are not an end unto themselves. In some cases organizations have formal corrective action processes that are used almost "by exception." When asked about this situation, they reply that process improvement teams, managed outside the formal quality management system, deal with the "real" problems. While this arrangement may make sense to some, it often causes duplication of effort, multiple lists of improvement projects, and wasted time. Keeping things together is better.

The art and science of effective corrective action implementation require training in the use of the proper tools and provide the resources to pursue meaningful corrective action.

Basic corrective action implementation tools that should be understood and used by everyone in the organization include:

- Flow diagrams/process maps
- Cause-and-effect diagrams
- Check sheets
- Pareto analysis
- Calculation of averages
- Variation analysis
- Run charts
- Brainstorming
- Histograms
- Process capability studies

If everyone in the organization had training and was encouraged to use these simple tools, corrective action in many organizations would be greatly facilitated.

Beyond the basic tools, many tools can be learned by individuals or groups in an organization to enhance the ability to perform meaningful corrective action. We do not advocate teaching advanced analysis tools to everyone, but rather to a select small group (or perhaps one individual) that will have the opportunity to use them and who can develop some skill in their use. The tools of analysis are many, and there are literally hundreds of books available describing them. In addition to the tools previously mentioned, statistical analysis tools the authors have found helpful include:

- Scatter plots
- Control charts and precontrol charts
- Process capability analysis
- Correlation/regression analysis
- Design of experiments (DOE) in any of many forms
- Statistical process control (SPC) in its many forms
- Nonparametric statistical analysis
- Sampling
- Benchmarking

Powerful tools in the hands of poorly trained individuals can be dangerous. It's better to use simple tools well than powerful tools poorly. In addition, each organization should work toward having at least one "master" of the problem-solving process and tools. That person can be brought into situations requiring more detailed analysis. If they are assigned to the right projects and well supported, such experts are worth much more than the salary they are paid.

It is not uncommon to have such a master (a statistician?) as a member of the quality function, but this structure is not the norm. The master can functionally report anywhere in the organization, provided his or her role and responsibilities are clear.

The master needs to know four things about the tools:

1. How to correctly use each tool

2. Which tools to use in a given situation

3. The order in which the tools should be used

4. How to help others use the tools properly

In changing the thinking on corrective action, management must lead the way—provide the direction, establish the expectations, provide the resources, and review the results.

PREVENTIVE ACTION—A FORMAL MANAGEMENT ACTIVITY

It is interesting how many organizations resist any formal effort to address preventive action. In fact, some organizations search through their corrective actions to find a few to call preventive just to satisfy auditors. Preventive action is not working on problems that have already happened. Rather, it is looking to what could happen. It seems obvious that "an ounce of preventive action is much less expensive than a pound of corrective action." So why do organizations resist? Perhaps it is that even under the best of circumstances, preventing every problem and nonconformity would be exorbitantly expensive. In fact, it is probably impossible! So organizations just trust to luck instead of thinking through opportunities to spend a very little to preclude disasters.

To illustrate how an organization with a preventive action mentality could approach a particular issue, see Table 7.8.

Table 7.8   Correction, corrective action, and preventive action.

Issue	Correction	Possible corrective action	Possible preventive action
Customer complains about teller error on deposit transaction	Reverse erroneous transaction	Review and revise training process	Develop software to prevent invalid transactions from bring executed
Customer complains that there are no towels in hotel room	Manager sends towels	Institute use of checklist for housekeepers	Revise training process; institute use of visuals; bonus scheme for minimizing customer complaints
Machined parts are found to be oversized	Hone the parts	Provide go/no-go gages; initiate use of precontrol and control chart methods;	Initiate periodic machine capability studies; consider part redesign; revise preventive maintenance process

It should be evident that the actions taken for correction are considerably different from those for corrective action (and usually much easier to implement). And actions related to preventive action are much different than those to address corrective action (with corrective action typically "easier" to implement than preventive action).

At the very least, organizations should include preventive action as a regular and formal item of discussion at operations review meetings and management review meetings. Leaders need to have a forum and a process for managing the risk that things will go wrong.

PREVENTIVE ACTION—PROCESSES

The preventive action concept is most effective when applied during process development. For more detailed information, see Chapter 5.

PREVENTIVE ACTION—RISK ASSESSMENT AND MITIGATION

In addition to formal discussions in management meetings, it is also desirable for management to promote the consideration of preventive action in the product design and development phase and when new processes are being developed.

Techniques and tools for evaluating preventive action opportunities include:

- FMEA and FMECA (failure modes and effects analysis and failure modes, effects and criticality analysis)[2]

- MTBF (mean time between failure) and MTTR (mean time to repair) analysis

- Fault tree analysis

- Product/system availability analysis

- Flowcharts

- Experimental design

These techniques and tools can be useful in evaluating and making cost and performance trade-offs for products and mitigating risk associated with product performance (for example, warranty claims, loss of good will) and liability exposure. The latter issue alone can make a compelling case for an aggressive preventive action process in many organizations.

PREVENTIVE ACTION—CHAOS, COMPLEXITY, AND SIMPLE SOLUTIONS

We have all implemented process changes that add new controls or process steps. There may have been significant debate about the cost of the new resources, but suppose everyone agreed that the additional controls or resources would improve process output. In many cases we were surprised to find that the behavior of the process did not get better. It not only got worse but also became less predictable. The problem or potential problem we set out to solve is gone. But other, new problems abound. Why?

Every step, control, or resource added to a process increases complexity. If we add enough of them, the behavior of the process is very likely to become chaotic. We have all observed this, but it is easy to forget that there are mathematical reasons for this behavior.[3] It is the way complex processes naturally behave!

One reason for this is related to the number of interactions among the steps, resources, and controls. In Chapter 5 we pointed out that it is important to simplify the interactions among the processes of the quality management system. The same thing is true within each process. In a 1990 *Quality Progress* article, Bruce McGill explained it this way:

> Each element added to a process increases the chaos in the process. If the process has three elements, there are three interactions. If it has four elements, there are six interactions. With five elements, you get 10 interactions, and so on. The number of interactions increases at a much faster rate than the number of elements.
>
> We have been told that the way to keep our processes in control is to eliminate special causes.[4] The way we often do that is to provide resources. If we find a special cause, we add a piece of equipment, a person, or a method to try to eliminate that cause. What we have really done is to make the process more complex and increase the number of interactions.
>
> The caveat against adding resources to fix a problem is nothing new. We have been told for some time that any resource that doesn't add value for the customer should be eliminated. What is new is the reason for the caveat. The current wisdom says that we shouldn't add resources because the direct cost of those resources adds to the cost of producing the product. Since it doesn't add value to the product, there can be no corresponding increase in the sales price. As a result profits are reduced.
>
> Chaos says that there is an even more compelling reason for the caveat. It says that the addition of resources adds complexity to

the process and therefore may destabilize it. It is relatively easy to calculate the direct cost of adding a resource. It is almost impossible to calculate the indirect cost of the additional complexity.[5]

It is noteworthy that the McGill article was published in 1990 and we continue to see resources added to solve problems. This is in spite of the great emphasis on lean manufacturing techniques and their spread from manufacturing to service organizations.

From the viewpoint of prevention of nonconformity or undesirable process performance, then, it is very worthwhile to consider simplifying processes.

PREVENTIVE ACTION—ANTICIPATING AND MANAGING UNCERTAINTY

Uncertainty is a reality of life for all organizations. Conventional wisdom is to address uncertainty by use of decision trees, contingency planning, risk management techniques (as described elsewhere in this chapter), planning tools (Gantt charts, CPM, PERT charts) or a variety of other conventional management techniques. Yet, uncertainty plagues organizations, and the results are outcomes such as development projects that fail, manufacturing processes that do not generate planned output, or people who do not perform as expected.

Often the cause of the undesired outcome is the result of the failure of the organization to recognize that different types of uncertainty exist, and that to minimize the impact of uncertainty, several management approaches may be required, depending on the nature of uncertainty.

We suggest that *a preventive action process that recognizes the many faces of uncertainty can be a powerful force in mitigating the impact of uncertainty on organizational performance.*

In an article in the *MIT Sloan Management Review,*[6] uncertainty was characterized in terms of four types: process variation, foreseen uncertainty, unforeseen uncertainty, and chaos. In any organization, all of these forms exist, some more than others, depending on such factors as the nature of the organization, its products, its culture, and the markets it serves.

The most typical organizational approach to formally addressing uncertainty, if at all, is to consider the variation dimension, and perhaps to a lesser degree, foreseen uncertainty.

From a preventive action viewpoint, we suggest that it would be worthwhile to adopt a process that categorizes the uncertainty that the organization faces in the broadest terms, identifies the most significant categories and develops preventive action plans to address the predominant forms of uncertainty.

For example, in manufacturing processes, variation may be the predominant form of uncertainty. In this case, training managers on tools and techniques for identification and elimination of special causes of variation may be appropriate and sufficient. If however, foreseen uncertainty is dominant, (for example, for organizations requiring Food and Drug Administration approval of new drugs), perhaps emphasis on contingency planning training or the use of decision trees would be more appropriate. For organizations frequently facing unforeseen uncertainty (for example, an army conducting a military mission), conventional tools such as PERT charts are relatively useless; much more high-level thinking is required, such as the use of iterative external scans of the environment to uncover potential opportunities and threats, which could be incorporated quickly into strategy and tactics. In a chaotic environment (perhaps a dot-com startup), access to financial resources and ability to make instantaneous decisions may be critical.

It is interesting to note that depending on the circumstances and the nature of uncertainty faced by the organization, the leaders may, as a preventive action, need to migrate training and competence development from traditional "variation reduction tools and techniques" (for example, SPC) to a management process more heavily dependent on learning and entrepreneurial skills.

Creatively managing uncertainty is not a mainstream preventive action concept, but it is one that the authors strongly suggest for consideration for organizations that are committed to going beyond the minimum. Such a unique approach to preventive action has the potential to produce exceptional results.

WHAT CAN I DO NOW?

Make a quick assessment of how well corrective action and preventive action is done in your organization. Are the differences among correction, corrective action, and preventive action understood across the organization?

- Has your organization invested in training all levels of personnel in the art and science of corrective action?

- Is corrective action, when implemented, institutionalized to ensure long-lasting process improvement?

- Look at what people are recording on corrective action request forms. How would you characterize the contents of these forms (trivial excuses like "warn the operator" or real cause correction)?

- Look at what people are recording on preventive action forms. How would you characterize them?

- Is there evidence that preventive action in the form of risk assessment is integrated into the design process (where applicable)?

- Do you formally consider how to simplify processes? If not, should you? If you do, are you being effective?

- How do you manage the uncertainties that face your organization?

- Look at implementation of solutions. Does your organization often find the cause but cannot or does not correct it?

The changes you might need to make in the corrective action or preventive action process may be a longer-term effort, especially if there is an organizational culture to overcome.

8

Change the Way You Audit

"Tempora mutantur, nos et mutamur in illis."
("Times change, and we change with them too.")

Owen
Epigrammata (1615)

A common approach to internal quality auditing is to assign this activity to the quality department, which assigns a few individuals to perform the quality audits for the organization. This approach is reasonable if the purpose of internal quality audit is solely to assess compliance with requirements. If, however, the organization has an expectation that the quality management system should contribute to performance improvement and customer satisfaction, then auditing for just compliance is not sufficient.

We need to change the way we think about the internal auditing process if we want to get the best return on our auditing investment.

But before we contemplate how to change the way we think, let's first consider a few definitions. Table 8.1 gives the ISO 9000:2000 definition of audit.

Table 8.1 Definition of "audit."

Audit—Systematic, independent, and documented process for obtaining audit evidence and evaluating it objectively to determine the extent to which audit criteria are fulfilled.

Source: ANSI/ISO/ASQ Q9000:2000.

The Note to the ISO definition describes an internal audit as follows:

Internal audit—Sometimes called a first-party audit, is conducted by, or on behalf of, the organization itself for internal purposes. . . .

These definitions are flexible and useful. And it is interesting to note that they do not mention quality. Let's examine the definitions.

Auditing is a process:

- For *obtaining evidence* (facts supported by credible data) related to the system, process, area, subject, or activity being audited

- For *determining* the *extent* to which the system, *process,* area, subject, or activity being audited *meets* some *specified criteria*

- That is *conducted objectively* and *impartially*

This definition provides a starting point for many of the concepts needed to manage and conduct audits for maximum organizational benefit.

WHY AUDIT?

Why do organizations conduct internal quality audits? Many organizations just don't get it. They conduct internal quality audits because ISO 9001 requires them and for no other reason. And the managers of these organizations have no expectations of the audit process beyond determining if the organization is complying with ISO 9001 requirements and, in particular, if it is fulfilling the requirements of clause 8.2.2 in the least disruptive manner possible.

Over the years, managers, and in particular top managers, have never embraced the concept of auditing with the same fervor as they have embraced other management tools such as Six Sigma, lean manufacturing, TQM, and SPC. The reasoning seems strange since the general concept of auditing is firmly embedded in management thinking. Most organizations retain financial auditors, both internal and external. In simplistic terms, the financial auditors look back over a period of time to ensure the books have been handled in accordance with generally accepted accounting principles (GAAP). Of course, the books may have no direct relationship with either the product or service delivered to customers or to where the organization will be tomorrow, next month, or next year. The paradox is that management accepts, and even embraces, financial auditing, which appears to have its focus on the health of the books and what happened yesterday. But top management has not embraced quality auditing, which is focused on the health of the products and services the organization delivers to customers, and is forward-looking in terms of ensuring our processes remain capable of delivering products and services that meet or exceed customer expectations.

And many of these same organizations claim to place high value on "customer satisfaction" and claim to be customer-focused.

So we suggest that top managers should revisit the issue of what should be expected of the internal quality audit process. They need to decide how to organize and operate the process to be more than just a passive activity. The quality professionals likewise need to provide substantive justification for the investment in a proactive internal auditing process, remembering that the language of management is money.

So, why do we audit and what can we do beyond auditing to ensure compliance?

There are many reasons to perform internal quality audits:

- Meet requirements of ISO 9001 and ensure conformance to requirements.

- Seek opportunities to improve efficiency.

- Identify best practices that can be used elsewhere in the organization.

- Spread good ideas through auditors.

- Enhance organizational consistency.

- Intensify the focus on customer satisfaction throughout the organization.

- Ensure that there is alignment throughout the organization of objectives, operations, and activities with the quality policy.

- Determine if processes are being managed to ensure the organization's objectives will be met.

The first of these reasons is a nonissue. Any respectable organization that desires to have at least a minimally acceptable quality management system must have an audit process in place. But the other potential reasons on the list are not ISO 9001 requirements. Rather, they are characteristics of auditing that go beyond the minimum. They are characteristics of audit-related processes that can greatly enhance the contribution of quality auditing to the organization.

It is these other potential reasons to audit that we encourage organizations to consider. Incorporating some or all of these concepts into the internal audit process will result in business performance improvement.

Let's look closer at these reasons or potential reasons to audit.

Meet Requirements of ISO 9001 and Ensure Conformance to Requirements

The most basic reason for quality auditing is to ensure conformance to requirements, and this seems to be well understood and addressed in most organizations, since it is an ISO 9001 requirement. But organizations should expect conformity with requirements to be the outcome of a mature QMS. Perhaps when a quality management system is new there may be issues with compliance, but over time the expectation should be that all processes will conform to requirements.

If we audit only to assess conformity, it is not hard to understand why top managers often question the value added or return on the investment from auditing. If we go beyond the minimum and take the additional step of quantifying the results, the value question will evaporate. If we focus on determining how well we are meeting customer requirements rather than just how well we conform to ISO 9001, we emphasize the importance of the customer and improvement of internal operations.

HOW INTERNAL AUDITS CAN BE DIFFERENT— GOING BEYOND

Many organizations stop with auditing for conformity. Perhaps the reasoning is "that's what the registrar's auditors do." And this is true. Registrars' auditors cannot go beyond conformity because in doing so they would be considered to be acting as consultants or overstepping ethical boundaries. Internal auditors have fewer constraints. They can be expected to act as the "eyes and ears of top management." They can delve deep into processes, looking for ways to eliminate waste in addition to looking for conformity. They can look at the system and determine if it is achieving needed outcomes—if it is effective at meeting objectives. It is going beyond auditing for conformity that can render internal audits invaluable.[1]

Going Beyond—Seek Opportunities to Improve Efficiency

If the organization selects "the best and brightest" of its staff to be quality auditors (more on this later), then it is not unreasonable to expect the auditors to look carefully and critically at how the processes could run more efficiently or effectively. Fresh outside eyes looking at a process often see opportunities not apparent to those who are in the environment daily. There is a caution here, however, in that *outsiders,* when auditing, cannot possibly know all the reasons that processes operate as they do. So it is wise to train auditors to address areas for possible improvement as ideas to consider rather than as recommendations for specific action. Auditors need to be trained to respect the responsibility of the auditees to manage their processes. Auditors are neither police nor consultants; rather, *they are individuals on the same team* as the auditees with an overall responsibility to contribute to the implementation of more efficient and effective processes.

Going Beyond—Identify Best Practices

It is common for auditors to see best practices. It is beneficial to train auditors to look for best practices, so that we can replicate such practices in other areas of the organization. If we do not make the identification of best practices a management expectation of auditing, it will not happen. If it is an expectation, surprising positive results often occur. Transferring best practices to other parts of the organization is often very difficult, and the success of the transfer depends on the auditee providing a significant amount of help. The auditor needs to be sure the auditee is willing to provide this help before including a reference to best practices in the audit report.

Going Beyond—Spread Good Ideas

The organization can train auditors to keep their eyes open for approaches or techniques used by an auditee that would help the auditors in managing or working in their primary areas of responsibility or elsewhere. Also, internal auditors can suggest that the auditee consider approaches or techniques used elsewhere in the organization that may be applicable in the area being audited. It has been demonstrated in organizations that make knowledge transfer an auditing expectation that such cross-fertilization of knowledge and practices improves operational performance. Improved teamwork is an ancillary benefit.

Going Beyond—Enhance Organizational Consistency

Organizations can also train auditors to look for consistency across the organization. For example, if retail customer service activities are standardized for all stores in the chain, customers will receive more consistent service. If data collection methods are consistent across the organization, data analysis can be facilitated. If terminology is consistent, improvement may be facilitated. If documentation file structures are consistent, it is easier for personnel to find information. If assessment of competence by managers is consistent, personnel issues are easier to handle.

Going Beyond—Intensify the Focus on Customer Satisfaction

Properly trained auditors can determine if everyone in the organization is truly customer focused, or if customer focus is a management slogan with no basis in fact. It is absolutely acceptable, and desirable, for auditors to comment on the degree to which the area being audited is sensitive to internal and external customer satisfaction, especially if customer satisfaction is a tenet of the quality policy of the organization.

Auditors should also be trained to look for direct or indirect measures that relate to achieving customer satisfaction? If internal auditors raise the issue of how every element of the organization contributes to customer satisfaction, the audit function can be both a dynamic contributor to reinforcing a true customer-focused culture throughout the organization and a change-agent to establish such a culture.

Going Beyond—Ensure That There is Alignment Throughout the Organization

Even though the process approach has been widely discussed since the release of ISO 9001:2000, the concept of aligning all elements of an organization with its overall objectives and quality policy is frequently applied inconsistently. It is not uncommon for auditors to receive a blank stare from auditees when the internal auditor asks, "How does this operation support the achievement of the quality policy and quality objectives?" By asking such a question, internal auditors can expand awareness of alignment to the entire organization.

Going Beyond—Determine If Processes Are Being Managed to Ensure the Organization's Objectives Will Be Met

When asking questions related to process performance in any area, auditors should explore how the area or activity measures key performance indicators. They should ask about how data are being used to ensure process performance, product conformance, and achievement of the overall objectives of the organization. Auditors can reinforce the importance of measurement, data analysis, and the importance of continual attention to improvement throughout the organization.

TRAIN THE AUDITORS TO GO BEYOND

We cannot expect auditors to make recommendations for improvement if they do not fully understand it! Auditors should receive training in the tools such as:

- Workplace organization, simplification, and cleanliness
- Basic quality tools
- Process management
- Systems thinking

- Waste elimination

- Basic statistics

It is not possible for all auditors to know everything about such tools, but there should be at least one master auditor on staff who does know most of it.

STRUCTURING THE AUDIT PROCESS

The internal audit process can be a powerful tool to drive improvement and satisfaction. But such results do not occur by chance. We mentioned above, for example, that auditors need to be bright. *Organizations should select only the best and the brightest to be auditors.* Having talented people performing audits maximizes the quality of thought in the identification of best practices, in seeking out opportunities for improvement, in assessing dedication to customer satisfaction, and in judging the degree to which the area being audited embraces the process approach.

Also having highly regarded individuals performing audits sends a message to the organization that auditing is important. It is not an activity to be grudgingly tolerated. It is not a policing activity. Rather, it is important enough to the organization that highly regarded individuals are assigned to this activity.

It is often argued that an organization cannot afford to have the best and the brightest as auditors because of the amount of time required to perform audits. "We cannot take our top people off their jobs to have them spend their time doing audits," is the often-heard claim. To address this concern, we propose that the organization consider an approach to auditing that establishes two kinds of audits:

- Broad audits that cut across all elements of the organization (for example, establishing and maintaining a competent workforce)

- Audits of limited scope that investigate one specific process or area

We call the broad-scope audits horizontal audits and limited-scope audits vertical audits. Examples of these concepts are shown in Table 8.2.

By getting the best and brightest to be part-time auditors, we can "walk the middle ground" of having a vibrant audit process that involves the best brain power in the organization, while not creating an overwhelming time burden on the part-time auditing staff. It is typical for these part-time auditors to conduct one audit per quarter with a total time commitment of one day per quarter. Such an approach has proven very effective in a variety of

Table 8.2 Broad- and limited-scope audits.

Horizontal audits (broad scope)	Vertical audits (limited scope)
Competence across the organization (3 days)	Printed wiring assembly solder process (2 hours)
Quality policy and objectives deployment (4 days)	Second-floor housekeeping (1.5 hours)

manufacturing and services organizations, especially when part-time auditors work in teams.

TACTICS TO MAXIMIZE THE VALUE OF THE AUDIT PROCESS

Two additional aspects of the internal audit process can be exploited by an organization. The first relates to the potential contribution that can result when the administrator of the audit process reviews and analyzes all internal audit results for trends or recurring problem areas. The second relates to the use of the audit process to check for the alignment of objectives and policy throughout the organization.

Review and Analysis of Audit Results

The review and analysis aspect of audit program management is often ignored or informally performed. Top managers should ensure there is someone responsible (for example, the administrator of the audit process) for systematically reviewing the audit reports collectively and looking for trends or opportunities for improvement that may not be obvious from individual audit reports. Suppose, for example, that in a review of 10 recent audits there is a recurring problem with failure to analyze process or product data. The reviewer may recommend that a problem-solving team be established to determine the true cause of the problem. Or perhaps the reviewer noticed that there are several findings for instruments being out of service or having calibration schedules extended because of problems with an outside calibration lab. The reviewer could recommend a supplier audit of the lab to determine the cause of the problem and possible solutions. Or perhaps the reviewer does not see evidence that internal audits are concentrating on measuring process performance and analyzing results. This could point out a need for improvement in the audit program itself or it could mean there is a need for auditor training. Reviewers should make recommendations that stimulate correction of problem causes. They should avoid recommending training, procedure modification, or other specific corrective actions unless the cause is clearly known.

Also, since organizations may be performing several kinds of audits, the data obtained may be quite diverse. The reviewer should consider use of a variety of tools to analyze the data generated from internal audits. For example, use of graphs and charts, histograms, Pareto charts, cause-and-effect diagrams, and simple calculations of averages and dispersion (i.e., variance) may be appropriate when attempting to extract information from a composite database of internal audit results.

The management review process is an ideal forum for presenting the results of these reviews. Several linked requirements embedded in ISO 9001:2000 point to the use of management review to drive improvement in the organization. These requirements include Clause 8.4, requiring analysis of data; Clause 8.5.1, requiring continual improvement of the quality management system through use of audit results as well as other actions; and Clauses 5.6.1 and 5.6.2, which require top management to consider inputs from the results of audits to ensure continuing quality management system suitability and to seek opportunities for improvement. These linked requirements are discussed in more detail in Chapter 6 and are shown in Figure 6.1.

The analysis process can be expanded if the organization has a single database for problems, corrective actions, and audit findings. In such cases, the reviewer can extend the analysis to compare audit data with other information. This can aid in identifying the most significant opportunities.

Analysis of audit results can indeed be a powerful input for positive change in the organization. If the analysis is done well, it will positively influence performance improvement by taking the audit process beyond minimum requirements and exploiting its potential.

Auditing to Assess Alignment of Organization Policy and Objectives

Alignment and how it is achieved were discussed in detail in Chapter 4. If top management sets the expectation for auditors to look for alignment, this aspect of managing will be reinforced. Such attention is helpful when auditing detailed product realization subprocesses, where it is easy to become mired with operational details and lose sight of an overall objective like dedication to satisfying the end-customer.

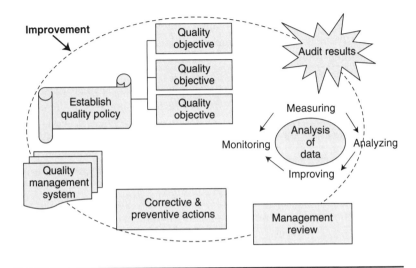

Figure 8.1   The improvement loop.

AUDIT RESULTS AND CORRECTIVE ACTION

In addition there should be a close coupling between the identification of nonconformities in the internal audit process and the corrective action process. In many organizations the audit administrator is also responsible for maintaining the corrective action databases and for ensuring that corrective action is implemented, that it is effective, and that it is institutionalized by documentation changes, training and reaudit, as appropriate. In many organizations, auditors even generate requests for corrective action, as appropriate, as an output of an audit.

The interrelationship of audit, corrective action, and management reviews is shown in Figure 8.1.

HOW TO JUSTIFY INVESTMENT IN A ROBUST INTERNAL AUDIT PROCESS

There are many opportunities to demonstrate how the audit process contributes to customer satisfaction and operational efficiency (profit enhancement in for-profit organizations and more cost-effective operations for not-for-profit organizations). To the extent practical, issues used to communicate information related to the audit process should be framed in monetary terms. This is a real necessity when the information is intended for top managers. For example, rather than stating, "We have a continuing issue with nonconforming product in Department A. This has been identified in each of the past three audits of this area." The audit administrator could state that "Nonconforming product from Department A, observed over the past nine months, has resulted in excess cost of $234,873 as measured by Finance." To the extent possible, audit reports should always communicate audit results in the language of management, which is data related to cost, production, risk, and money.

When facts are presented to managers in a language that is easy for them to understand (lost customers, wasted resources, rework, and money), action to address a situation is more likely to occur. By being attentive to how internal audit information is communicated around the organization, the auditors can profoundly influence the allocation of resources to improve performance of important activities.

Top managers review all audits and will be sensitive to anything that is characterized in monetary terms.

Some areas where auditors and audit administrators can be sensitive to possibilities for quantifying impacts include:

- **Process inputs (from both internal and external suppliers)**—Are process inputs measured, and, if so, do they meet requirements? If not, what is the financial impact? The impact can be stated in terms of lost time due to either rework or late delivery.

- **Process outputs**—What is the output of the process being audited? Are there yield issues? If so, what does an X percent level of nonconforming product or service convert to when measured in terms of cost to correct (for example, rework and reverification costs in manufacturing, or correction costs in service)? And what are the costs related to customer dissatisfaction (W. Edwards Deming reminds us that much of this cost is unknown and unknowable, but it is often more significant than the identifiable costs)? If the results of the process do not meet requirements and other internal objectives, what is an estimate of the financial impact?

- **Resources**—Resources include process equipment, measuring and monitoring equipment, information, people, and anything else that may be necessary to ensure effective operation of the process. Could new equipment make a significant improvement in efficiency or effectiveness? What will it cost? What will it save? Does it appear that we are doing things that do not add value? Where? How much?

- **Controls**—Processes must operate under controlled conditions. Could we invest in additional controls to effect a significant improvement in process stability? What would be the financial gain?

- **Process validation**—Is there evidence that processes may not be capable of consistently meeting specified requirements? Although ISO 9001 does not require process validation except for processes where the results cannot be verified after a product has been produced, would it improve operations if process capability were studied and improved?

  Can process validation enable us to eliminate institutionalized verification activities (such as inspection) without impacting quality? How much would be saved by eliminating such verification activities?

- **Competence of personnel**—Are personnel competent? Is there an obvious lack of ability, skills, training, or experience that affects process performance? What is the cost of a lack of competence? Most auditors have no business attempting to directly judge people's competence. Rather, they normally look at those things that make an individual competent. These include whether job requirements are being met for specific training, experience, education, or demonstrated skills. Auditors can be taught to be sensitive to levels of competence and to assess the abilities (physical and mental characteristics and education) and skills (training and practice) of audited personnel. And they need to use care and sensitivity when quantifying competence issues.

- **Interactions with other processes**—Often issues arise between organizations or processes, and these "between the cracks" issues can have significant financial impact. Auditors and audit reviewers should look for the economic effect of interface issues.

- **Process improvement**—Process improvement opportunities hold great potential for quantification. Auditors and audit administrators can often identify large potential economic benefits. They do so either by looking at processes that are underperforming with current methods, controls, and resources or by suggesting the consideration of alternative approaches.

LEADERS NEED TO TAKE ACTION

The internal quality audit process can contribute to and encourage both improvement and customer satisfaction. Top management has to want to capitalize on the potential of the audit process and to provide the resources to realize the potential benefits.

If top managers want to unlock the power of the internal audit process, the decision must be made to invest in the training of personnel and setting of expectations that go far beyond just assessing compliance. The audit process has the potential to make great contributions to the organization, but top managers need to change expectations and resource allocations.

WHAT CAN I DO NOW?

Review the internal audit process of your organization.

- Does it encourage the use of the best and the brightest individuals to be internal auditors?

- Does your organization invest in meaningful training to ensure auditor competence?

- Has your organization set expectations for auditors to identify opportunities for improvement and best practices that can be adapted to other areas of the organization, in addition to determining compliance? If not, what action should you take?

- Do you encourage auditors to check the area being audited to determine the degree of alignment of the area with the purpose and objectives of the organization?

- Do you encourage auditors to check for sensitivity to the requirements of the external customer?

- Do you include requirements for using the results of internal audits for consideration for improvement projects?

Does your organization analyze audit results periodically to identify and quantify opportunities for improvement? Is this process effective as a driver of performance improvement?

If the answer to any of the above questions is no or a qualified yes, what action should be taken?

9

Self-Assessment

*"The spirit of self-help is the root of all genuine growth in the individual;
and, exhibited in the lives of many, it constitutes the true source of
national vigor and strength."*

Samuel Smiles
Self-help (1859)

In the previous chapters we have presented strategies and concepts intended to improve business performance by expanding and enhancing basic quality management system elements.

This chapter introduces another role for the quality management system—a role that will enhance the ability of the organization to grow and prosper.

ISO 9001:2000 and ISO 9004:2000 are a consistent pair of standards. An organization can design and implement a quality management system to meet the minimum requirements as defined in ISO 9001. Either during or after that implementation, the organization can refer to ISO 9004 for ideas regarding how to expand the quality management system. The quality management system can be expanded both in breadth of application across the organization (for example, should we include the Finance Department in the scope) and in the depth to which it is applied. The purpose of this expanded breadth and depth is to achieve improved results.

ISO 9004 still has not received a rousing reception by the user community. A typical mentality has been to achieve compliance with ISO 9001 and then either do nothing further or look to other models for the pursuit of organizational excellence.

One feature of ISO 9004:2000 has received some favorable attention by the user community—Annex A, "Guidelines for Self-assessment." Self-assessment is one of the most effective processes an organization can use to drive improvement and customer satisfaction. It can also characterize both the maturity of the organization in specific areas (benchmarked against best practices) and the ability of an organization to continue to compete in the served market.

SELF-ASSESSMENT AND INTERNAL AUDIT— TWO DIFFERENT CONCEPTS

First, let's understand the difference between internal audit and self-assessment. Formal definitions are given in Table 9.1 and Table 9.2.

Table 9.1   Internal audit.

Internal audit—a systematic independent and documented process conducted for internal purposes to obtain audit evidence and evaluate it objectively to determine the extent to which audit criteria are fulfilled.

Developed from: ANSI/ISO/ASQ Q9000-2000.

Table 9.2   Self-assessment.

Self-assessment—a careful evaluation usually performed by, or at the direction of, the management of an organization that results in an opinion or judgment of the effectiveness and efficiency of the organization and the maturity of the quality management system.

Developed from: ANSI/ISO/ASQ Q9004-2000, Annex A.

Internal audits address the evaluation of whether existing policies, procedures, and requirements have been met. Even if we adopt the expanded view of auditing described in Chapter 8, we are still focused on identifying opportunities for improvement or best practices within the framework of the existing quality management system. Such actions are not judgments of process maturity—rather, they are observations that the process could be considered for improvement or that a practice in a particular area could be considered for implementation elsewhere in the organization.

WHY CONDUCT SELF-ASSESSMENTS

Self-assessment reveals the maturity of the quality management system or related processes, compared to some benchmark—such as a competitor, the Malcolm Baldrige National Quality Award (MBNQA) criteria, the European Foundation for Quality Management (EFQM) criteria, or the guidelines of ISO 9004. Self-assessment can also be used to appraise the degree to which prior changes in processes or systems have resulted in improved performance. Self-assessment can confirm that a process change has resulted in improvement or that additional work is required.

For organizations with a well-established quality management system, the Baldrige[1] model may be appropriate. But it is a daunting model for organizations with little experience with self-assessment. Just reading the Criteria for Performance Excellence brochure would trigger the pause response with prospective users.

Japan has long had the Criteria for the Deming Prize, which has been used to guide improvement of processes and performance. Another concept emerging from research in Japan is that if an organization desires to prosper in the long run, it needs to assess its use of innovation to make the changes that will ensure it can sustain its growth.[2]

The concept of self-assessment, then, appears to be a well-accepted process for judging the efficiency, effectiveness, and maturity of the quality management system. It can also be used by top management to determine the degree to which particular areas of presumed concentration (for example, lean and Six Sigma) are producing expected results.

Given the general recognition of the value of self-assessment, why is it not more widely used as a management tool? We offer a few thoughts based on experience with MBNQA, EFQM, and Deming approaches:

- Assessment and scoring systems are very complicated.

- Assessment takes a lot of time.

- Assessment requires extensive resources.

- The value of assessment is not well understood.

The predominant image of self-assessment in the user community is that of the Baldrige model. This may account for reluctance on the part of many organizations to consider implementing self-assessment processes.

CONDUCTING SELF-ASSESSMENTS

We recommend that organizations that have not yet performed self-assessment do so, using Annex A of ISO 9004:2000 as a model. We will provide a bit of detail that is not included in the annex.

Annex A of ISO 9004:2000 was developed to provide organizations with a simple, easy to use, and easy to understand approach for assessing the maturity of their quality management systems. The intention was also to make it easy to pinpoint areas where improvement may be needed and to provide insight into the relative priorities of the possible improvement projects.

The approach incorporated into Annex A sacrificed rigor and detail for ease of use and speed of implementation. It provides a way for organizations to start toward the excellence criteria without the overhead inherent to complex assessments.

The self-assessment approach described in Annex A could be applied as follows:

1. Create a scale of performance levels appropriate for the organization. The scale shown in Table 9.3 is a reasonable starting point.

2. Create an organizational profile giving the current business model and specifying the external (market, financial, and so on) conditions the organization expects to face in the next few years.

3. Use the profile as an aid to select the most important processes, functions, areas, divisions, or organizations to assess. Example: We might find that we should assess the preventive action processes.

4. Decide if the assessment is to be performed by an individual or a team.

5. Use ISO 9004:2000 to create a set of criteria for assessing the process, function, area, division, or organization. It is useful for the organization to also obtain and become familiar with the related criteria for the Malcolm Baldrige National Quality Award and the European Foundation for Quality Management. These may provide additional input for development of internal criteria. Sample criteria for the process selected could be as shown in Table 9.4.

6. Perform the assessment using the criteria established in step 5, using the maturity scale defined in step 1 to rate the maturity of the function for each criteria. Document the assessment in a table format similar to the assessment data sheet shown in Figure 9.1. Table 9.5 shows how the score was derived for the example in Figure 9.1.

7. Decide on improvement priorities and initiate a project to achieve the desired improvement.

Table 9.3 Self assessment scoring guide from 9004:2000.

Score	Performance Level	Guidance
1	No formal approach	No systematic approach evident, no results, poor results or unpredictable results
2	Reactive approach	Problem- or corrective-based systematic approach; minimum data on improvement results available
3	Stable formal approach	Systematic process-based approach, early stages of systematic improvements; data available on conformance to objectives and existence of improvement trends
4	Continual improvement emphasized	Improvement process in use; good results and sustained improvement trends
5	Best-in-class performance	Strongly integrated improvement process; best-in-class benchmarked results demonstrated

Source: ISO 9004:2000—Table A.1—Performance maturity levels.

Table 9.4 Developing assessment criteria.

Develop question 1:

    Process being assessed: Preventive action

    —Annex A question: How does management use preventive action for loss prevention?

    Question for our assessment: What process and sources of data are used to identify risks?

Develop other questions in similar manner

    Process being assessed: preventive action

    —Annex A question: _____

    Question for our assessment: _____

The seventh step is the most important. While the assessment results themselves may be useful, it is critical that you not treat every opportunity as having equal importance. This is the purpose of scoring. If a rigorous scoring process is used for each item in the criteria, you should get a great deal of information from the score. Table 9.6 gives scores for several criteria that were developed in the assessment of preventive action processes of an organization. From an analysis of these data an initial determination of action priorities can be made.

ISO 9004 Self-assessment
22 March 2002

Process being assessed: Preventive action

Annex A question: How does management use preventive action for loss prevention? (see ISO 9004:2000 Annex A Question 27 b)

Question
What process and sources of data are used to identify risks?

Answer to question

Design FMEAs are used to identify risks of field failures. Internal data on the process are the only source for identifying possible process failure risks. Customer feedback is not used. Risk of process problems is sometimes considered during management review, but lessons learned from earlier problems are seldom translated into preventive measures.

Strengths
+ Use of design FMEA has reduced product field failures.
+ Use of knowledge of operators and engineers to identify possible risks when designing new equipment or processes.

Areas for improvement
− Use customer requirements as a source of potential failure process risks.
− Use of a formal technique such as FMEA to identify potential risks of process failures.
− Increase the emphasis on risk management during management review.

Statement on Score
Improvement process used to identify product risks but process for identification of process risks not systematic.

Score 2.5

Figure 9.1 Assessment data sheet.

Table 9.5 Determining a score.

Statement on score

Improvement process used to identify product risks but process for identification of process risks not systematic.

2	Reactive approach	Problem—or corrective—based systematic approach; minimum data on improvement results available.
3	Stable formal approach	Systematic process—based approach, early stages of systematic improvements; data available on conformance to objectives and existence of improvement trends.

Score: 2.5 on a Scale of 1–5

Table 9.6 Tabulated scores for the process targeted for assessment.

Our example continued—summarize the scores

Target processes: preventive action

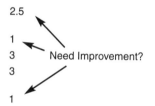

- What process and sources of data are used to identify risks?   2.5
- How are risks prioritized?   1
- How are decisions made on actions to take?   3   Need Improvement?
- How are preventive actions determined and implemented?   3
- How are the results of preventive actions measured and verified?   1

      Often it is important to display the scoring data so that they can be easily understood. One of the best ways to do this is to use the radar or spider chart technique illustrated in Figure 9.2.

      Self-assessment, as we indicated earlier, can be performed on individual processes or for entire organizations. As is true of any effort, the degree of top management involvement, support, and commitment will have a large impact on the value derived from the self-assessment.

      Small self-contained processes are best assessed by an individual or a small team. The assessment can be scoped to be completed in a few hours. Larger assessments—for example, the organization-wide process for setting objectives, monitoring performance, and closing competence gaps—could involve a larger team and take days, but not months.

      Also, analysis of the results of the assessments can take several forms. If a manager performed a self-assessment of his or her order-entry function,

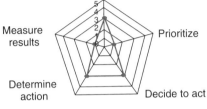

Figure 9.2   Graphical display of assessment data.

he or she could very well analyze the results and make decisions regarding improvement projects.

In the case of the organization-wide assessment of a process to manage objectives, performance, and competence, the entire team involved with the assessment could participate in the data-review and decision-making process.

The structure of the self-assessment process is not as important as conducting the assessment. It is far more effective to conduct a "ragged" self-assessment in a few hours and identify a few solid improvement opportunities than to agonize over formulating a perfect set of criteria and selecting the ideal assessment team.

Since there is a tendency to become obsessed with scoring (Baldrige scoring sometimes seems to be more important than the analysis of the issue), it should be noted that the scoring or rating of performance against criteria is not an absolute determiner of a course of action. Since all aspects of self-assessment contain an element of subjectivity, we suggest not becoming preoccupied with the precision of the ratings. *Use the information gathered from the assessment to guide the selection and prioritization of improvement projects.* Scoring is the beginning of prioritization and action.

PRIORITIZATION OF ACTIONS

The assessment results and scoring give us a first hint, but we need more data to determine what action we should take. First, we should develop brief statements of the various actions we could take and the benefits expected from each. Next we need to estimate the cost of doing each. Armed with this information, we are prepared to decide. Sometimes a simple ranking can be obtained by assigning a numerical value to the benefits and cost of each proposed action.

Assign a score to the benefits of each area for improvement:

- No benefit—1

- Small benefit in cost or customer satisfaction—2

- Moderate benefit in cost or customer satisfaction or both—3

- Large benefit in both cost and customer satisfaction—4

- Critical to business success—5

Assign a score to the implementation costs for each area for improvement:

- No or very low cost—5

- Small cost in both short and long term—4

- Small cost in short term and higher maintenance costs—3

- Moderate cost in short term but high maintenance costs—2

- High short- and long-term cost—1

If you assigned a benefit of 4 and a cost of 3 to an item, multiply the two and use Table 9.7 to guide prioritization.

As can be seen from Table 9.7, our score of 12 is in the area where it is probably good to take the proposed action. If the number had been a 9, 8, or 6, we would need to give the matter a great deal more study. It would be

---

Table 9.7   Prioritization tool.

One approach
Benefits

Cost		High 5	4	3	2	Low 1
Low	5	25	20	15	10	5
	4	20	16	12	8	4
	3	15	(12)	9	6	3
	2	10	8	6	4	2
High	1	5	4	3	2	1

Do it!   Think carefully!   Don't do it!

great if all our opportunities scored 20 or 25 with a very high ratio of estimated benefit to cost.

RELATIONSHIP TO MANAGEMENT REVIEW

Self-assessment is not a substitute for internal audit. As mentioned earlier, self-assessment and audit have different purposes. However, like internal audit results, the results of self-assessment should be fed into management review to enable top management to allocate resources and make decisions on priorities for improvement. Self-assessment input should be considered, discussed, and evaluated just like similar inputs to management review from customer complaints, process performance, and product conformity, and from the corrective action and preventive action processes.

Top management has the responsibility to weigh the significance of all the inputs to management review when making decisions regarding the quality management system. *It is not uncommon for the input from self-assessment to be of a more profound nature than many of the other QMS performance indicators.*

Self-assessment requires us to take a critical look at ourselves, to determine who we really are, and to decide what we want to be. It is then up to us to make the hard decisions to make the changes that will move the organization to the higher level we want to reach.

WHAT CAN I DO NOW?

Make a quick evaluation of the current degree of attention in the organization to self-assessment.

Does your organization use a self-assessment process? If not:

- Why not?

- Do you believe that performance of self-assessments would generate actionable information?

- Would the organization be willing to act on the outcome of self-assessments?

- What would be required to launch a self-assessment process?

If you do:

- Are results being used?

- Should your self-assessment be expanded?

10

Revitalize the Organization

"We pride ourselves on reinventing our own business model before somebody else does."

Michael Dell
Business 2.0[1]

The process management activities discussed in Chapter 5 and the improvement activities discussed in Chapter 6 can create and maintain a management system that is optimized to achieve the organization's objectives over the near term. That system also needs to be able to sense when changing conditions require major changes to maintain the organization's relevance in its market. This chapter will discuss recognizing the need for dramatic system changes, to use innovation to develop the changes that are needed and to consider the issues to be addressed prior to implementation of changes. The objective is to keep the organization and its quality management system relevant in the face of change.

LONG-TERM SUSTAINED GROWTH

Some organizations come and go; others are more lasting. Often the success of an organization is attributed to luck or the result of the actions of a particularly clever CEO. The authors believe that organizations that succeed over time have three characteristics:

- They are continually learning and growing.

- They have a way to determine the need to make basic changes in their products and management systems.

- They use innovation to make those changes.

In other words, they have the ability to achieve sustainable growth over long periods regardless of external forces like simultaneous pressures for vastly improved products at constantly declining selling prices. They remain competitive in spite of apparently unfavorable external conditions that drive their competitors out of business. They seem to thrive on innovation and change.

Long-term sustained growth depends on the organization's ability to continually do a number of things like:

- Use internal scans, self-assessment, and external scans to understand future requirements.

- Use innovation to understand future mission, vision, and strategies to meet new requirements.

- Change objectives, targets, and key processes to meet new needs.

- Prepare the workforce for inevitable changes.

- Implement, maintain, and improve a new quality management system to meet future requirements.

Figure 10.1 illustrates these and the related concepts that will be discussed in this chapter.

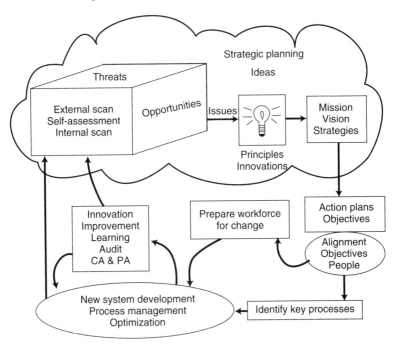

Figure 10.1   Keeping the quality management system relevant.

STRATEGIC PLANNING AND THE QUALITY MANAGEMENT SYSTEM

An essential element of long-term survival is planning for the future. But the strategic part of planning is often overlooked because of the emphasis on evaluating current and projected market conditions and forecasting short-term sales trends, revenues, and margins. These tactical activities may be needed, but they may only scratch the surface of future market conditions. A logical extension of the management system is to ensure that the organization has processes in place to understand the future market and business conditions it will face and to compare current and projected products and processes with that picture of the future.

This applies to more than just the organization's products and services. Organizations also need to plan changes to their quality management system to meet to meet future needs.

THE EXTERNAL SCAN

Organizations should first consider developing a statement of the envisioned external market impacts over the next several years and the relationship of those conditions to the organization. This is what planners call an "external scan" of both the market conditions and the circumstances that can affect the business environment. It can be conducted by developing answers to such basic questions as:

- What functions do my products provide for customers now?

- How will customers need or want that function to be provided three to five years from now?

- What products will we need in three to five years to provide that functionality?

- What will customers be willing to pay to get the needed or desired functionality in three to five years?

- What changes do we see coming in the legal and regulatory environment that will affect our business?

- Do we need to make *basic* changes in our product or its cost structure in the next three to five years?

- Do we need to make *basic* changes to our production or service delivery processes in the next three to five years?

- Do we need to make *basic* changes to our supporting processes in the next three to five years?

- When and how do we need to act on *basic* changes required for our products or processes?

Such questions should be answered periodically, and the conclusions drawn from the answers compared to those of the last few years. We need to be able to detect market changes that become apparent slowly. The sooner we detect a trend, the better able we will be to act on it and make certain that our organization remains relevant in the market. If we are fast enough in detecting basic market shifts, we may be able to make changes ahead of our competitors and thereby gain market share.

SELF-ASSESSMENT AND INTERNAL SCAN

Chapter 9 discusses self-assessment in detail. Some organizations use self-assessments to trigger change. Following this strategy, the results of self-assessment can highlight the need to change. But it is more common for organizations to be driven to fundamental change by external forces, to react to the impending crisis and ignore self-assessment. This can be a mistake. Even if the external forces that are driving change are well known, self-assessment can be a valuable aid for determining an appropriate action. If our external scan indicates a need to make basic changes, a next logical step is to conduct a self-assessment. Full self-assessments are not annual affairs. Most organizations conduct them every three to five years, but it is appropriate to perform an abbreviated version annually. We call this concept the "internal scan," and it should look at current key indicators of performance, as well as envisioned product and process issues.

This process needs to take into account the results of the external scan but it should not be considered as a secondary effort. When properly done it involves the systems thinking concepts described in Chapter 5. Top managers need to think about how the internal system interacts with the external world. The purpose is to identify changes needed to keep the system relevant under emerging conditions.

Ask the Right Questions

Planning implies development of action items to change in order to be successful in the future. But often action plans are based on the wrong information. The planning process inherently gets information relating to lots of questions. And the questions are far more important than the answers. The right answers to the wrong questions can send the organization on a disastrous course. If time is spent developing the right set of questions, the answers will be a guide to future success.

STRATEGIC THINKING

Performing external and internal scans requires strategic thinking. The consequences of ignoring strategic thinking can be serious. If we fail to detect a basic shift in customer needs or wants, our competitors may meet those needs and we may become completely irrelevant in that market. We could be forced out of business. At best we would need to play catch up to remain competitive.

Organizations are typically sensitive to determining the need to change their products, services, and processes. It is not so easy to know when to address overall change to the management system. The automobile industry serves as an example of this. For decades U.S. automakers changed models practically every year, but they were slow to recognize and react to the shift in attitude of the marketplace toward the quality of the vehicles delivered. When the need to improve quality became a crisis, the industry had to make basic changes.

As with products and individual processes, management systems can become stale, inflexible, or even irrelevant. Long-term success depends at least partially on the organization's recognizing when market shifts occur and acting in time to ensure survival, if not prosperity!

Once needed changes are identified, it is always worthwhile to revisit the organization's mission and vision statements. If the needed changes are truly significant, one or both of these may need to be revised.

THE DRIVERS OF CHANGE

The need for basic systemic change can be driven by several external and internal factors. The external factors include:

- **Changes in customer perception of the organization's products and services**—Competitors may improve their market share at our expense by changing customers' perceptions of their product and services vis-à-vis our products and services. Or, our actual performance may have declined. An organization may find that its management system is ill equipped to sense or understand this situation, much less address it.

- **Rapid changes in technology**—An organization may find itself in the situation in which technology is changing very rapidly.

- **Rapid changes in market conditions**—Such factors as e-commerce may be changing the way the customers expect to be able to purchase products and services.

- **Increasing regulatory requirements**—An organization participating in regulated markets may determine that new regulations could significantly reduce flexibility.

- **Deregulation**—An organization in a stable, highly structured market may find itself opened to unbridled competition.

- **Situations related to financing the organization**—Often organizations face increased pressure for improved return on investment to get loans or sell equity to finance ongoing operations and growth.

- **Pressures related to stock price and dividends**—Equity markets and stock analysts often demand real and perhaps unrealistic improvements in performance.

- **Direct pressure to change the management system**—The organization's whole industry may be moving to compliance with a management system standard such as ISO 9001 or customers may demand that suppliers become registered to ISO 9001.

- **Board of directors pressure**—Major changes requested by a BOD may well be based on data or perception of impending changes in the external environment.

Internal drivers of the need for basic change include:

- **Competitive advantage**—All organizations seek to achieve advantages over competitors, and top management may believe a better, faster, smarter management system may enable the organization to attract customers.

- **Self-assessment results**—Through review of the organization's internal self-assessment, top management may decide there is a need to make basic changes to the management system.

- **New markets**—Top mangers may perceive major opportunities in markets never before penetrated, and these markets may be half a world away.

- **New product lines**—If current markets are saturated and highly competitive, there may be a need to create whole new lines of products or services while maintaining growth of current offerings.

- **Related markets**—Top managers may perceive opportunities for growth in tangential markets for existing products

- **Product obsolescence**—It may be obvious that the organization's only products are like typewriters and slide rules; they will be replaced quickly with different items that perform the same function better and faster.

For most people in the organization, there is only one reality related to the drivers that are causing the organization to need change: There is nothing they can really do about them! If the changes are driven by external conditions, and most really are, even top managers can have little effect on these external forces; however, they need to have processes to sense them early and to address them swiftly.

WORKFORCE READINESS TO MAKE THE CHANGES

There are two aspects of workforce readiness to make changes: one is related to the emotional reaction that is experienced, and the other is related to workforce competence and related confidence. These two aspects are interrelated.

The emotional aspect is the easier of the two to address in the near term, and it is prudent to anticipate three kinds of reactions to the need for change:

- **Some people embrace changes**—They may perceive the change as being in their best interest, or they may just want to see the organization get better.

- **Some people will just "go along"**—They generally feel they have no say anyway, and whatever is best for the organization is OK with them.

- **Some people are hostile to change**—They may see it as disadvantaging them, feel threatened by change, or be uncomfortable with the uncertainty related to change, or they may feel that the change is just not in the best interest of the organization.

Top managers need to realize that the success of any change will depend on people. As the need to change emerges, the organization's objectives need to be realigned, as is discussed in Chapter 4, and the people need to be fully involved in this process. People need to be given information about the changes and the reasons they are needed. They need to be shown the data and information that were used in deciding on the changes. They will want to provide input, and top managers should take the time to listen. But the value of that input and the attitudes of the workforce members will depend to some extent on how well top managers have addressed the other aspect of workforce readiness: competence and confidence.

The time to begin to build the capacity of the workforce to absorb and implement major changes is long before changes are needed. Normally, people are better able to deal with changes when they have confidence in their competence to succeed. As the old saying goes, "If you think you can do it, you probably can; if you think you can't do it, you most likely can't." There is a need to develop competence by ensuring that the workforce has the education, training skills, and experience to meet the organization's needs. They also need the shared vision[2] discussed in Chapter 5, and the collective perception that by working together, they are competent enough to handle any challenge they will meet. The readiness of the workforce to accept and implement change can be determined by workforce surveys and self-assessment.

Shared Adversity and Shared Success

One way to achieve such confidence is through shared adversity that results in shared success. If in stable times, the workforce is given challenging but attainable goals and has worked in teams to meet those challenges, it should be well positioned to take on more dynamic challenges. Workers will have learned to innovate together to meet challenges. The key is the word "learn." When teams do projects to make small improvements, the improvements are not the only result; another result is the learning that takes place and the confidence that learning brings. We often hear arguments such as, "Continual improvement is not important because we have optimized the process and we don't want them (the workers) messing around with it." Such arguments and the banning of innovative improvement can doom an organization the next time revitalization is needed. Alternatively, *engaging employees in teams to perform many small improvement projects is an excellent approach to building overall employee confidence and competence. Confidence-building can result from successfully completing many small projects that are conducted in good, stable times.* So start preparing the workforce now!

Innovation, the Engine of Success

Preparing the workforce for change also requires that the organization take advantage of people's innovative abilities. It means that leaders in the organization need to seek out new and innovative ideas. They need to identify the people who have the intelligence, knowledge, experience, and willingness to develop new and innovative ideas.

Action plan

The result of all this assessment and planning should be action plans to carry the organization through changes. If your organization has already accomplished the actions outlined in Chapters 1–9, the organization's action plans might describe how you will do those things all over again! The action plans describe what will be done to review organizational basics (principles, mission, and vision), to reevaluate the organization's objectives, to determine what processes will be the keys to achieving the future vision, and to reoptimize processes. Action planning is an inherent activity of the organization's top managers, but it needs to be coordinated and supported at the appropriate levels to ensure buy-in and alignment. Indeed, top managers may conceive wonderful plans, but it is others in the organization that will do the implementing.

REVIEW ORGANIZATIONAL BASICS

The action plan normally assigns the review of organizational basics to top management, and sometimes it is viewed as a part of the strategic planning process. It includes:

- Review of the organization's basic principles against needs for the future. Chapter 1 discusses principles.

- Review of the organization's formal mission. If there is a basic shift in product strategies, there may be a need to make a major change in the organization's formal stated purpose or mission.

- Review of the organization's formal vision of the future. While the basic mission of the organization may remain the same for very long periods, the stated vision can be less static. If basic changes are projected over the next few years, the vision statement should probably be updated to reflect this expectation.

- Review of the organization's basic business model. Considering the major changes that are needed, this activity needs to describe how the organization will achieve adequate financial results. This may be a relatively simple assessment of the projected return on the investment required to make the changes, or it may require a basic revision to the organization's business model.

REEVALUATE THE ORGANIZATION'S OBJECTIVES AND ALIGNMENT

The action plan should assign responsibilities for review of the organization's objectives. If major changes are needed, there is normally a need to revise the formal organizational objectives and establish new measures and targets. The organization will need to change its objectives to reflect results that are needed to meet the new future vision. Establishment of organizational objectives and ensuring alignment are activities that can be done only by the organization's top managers. But top managers cannot do this alone; they must involve the appropriate functional leaders, supervisors, and to an appropriate extent, the workers. Establishment and alignment of objectives are discussed in Chapter 4.

DETERMINE, DEVELOP, AND MANAGE THE NEW KEY PROCESSES

The action plan needs to describe how the organization will identify processes most important to making change, meeting the new vision, and achieving the new objectives. This work should also start with top managers but, as with determining measures and targets, it needs to also involve others at appropriate levels. Most organizations will have already determined key processes that are appropriate for the current conditions. The issue here is to determine which processes are important to achieving the vision and the needed future results. The action plan also needs to describe responsibility for development of these processes and integration with other system processes so that the system is reoptimized to meet its new objectives.

WHAT CAN I DO NOW?

There is an old saying: "Plan well but don't plan forever; for without action all planning is useless." Most of this chapter is about planning because without a good plan, organizations often take the wrong action. The most important aspect of the planning is the determination of the key processes. If this is done correctly, then the organization's time and money to optimize them will be well spent. If it is not done right, not only will money be wasted, but also time will be lost. If this part of the planning is not correct, there could be dire consequences for the organization. If it is done correctly, there is high probability for long-term success.

Is your organization thinking about the future? If you believe you should, you can ask yourselves a few questions:

- How are you planning for the future?

- How will your QMS be structured?

- What is your timetable for changing to accommodate anticipated changes in the marketplace? What are the implications for how you ensure the quality of our products and services?

- How is your quality strategic thinking aligned with and integrated into the strategic thinking of the organization?

The answers to these and related questions are not easy to obtain, but they may be the most important contribution a quality professional can make to an organization.

Reflections

"I will take the ring . . . although I do not know the way."

J. R. R. Tolkien
TheFellowship of the Ring

This book has been about change. Changing the way managers think about their business, about quality, about processes, about systems, and about achieving results. We have explored a number of things you can do to build a more effective quality management system to achieve business results. By now you have considered a number of actions you could take. Step back now and think about your role in actually affecting change.

TIMING

There is a time for everything. A time to change and a time to stay the course; a time to drive improvement and a time to wait for opportunities; a time. . . . We all need to recognize that timing is critical. If you have a receptive organization, boss, or culture, the time to move may be now.

PARTS OF THE ORGANIZATION ARE AT DIFFERENT LEVELS OF READINESS TO CHANGE

Some parts of your organization may have a culture that already demands change and improvement while other areas of the organization are headed by leaders who impede changes their subordinates would embrace. Other areas may be totally resistant to change. You may want to make a map of your organization that shows the readiness in each key area. It makes the most sense to work first with the parts of the organization that are the most receptive. This means that you may need to avoid working with the parts of the organization that need the most improvement and help.

DO LESS AND GET MORE DONE

Whether you are a quality professional, an executive, or an employee working elsewhere in an organization, there is no way you can implement change by yourself. The quality professional needs to lead by facilitating change. The executive must be engaged but has to delegate effectively. If you work elsewhere in the organization, your ability to create change is limited only by your initiative and creativity. Reflect on your role. Is it clear to you and well defined for others?

DO THE THINGS YOU KNOW
YOU KNOW HOW TO DO

There is an old saying that the wise man is not he who knows but rather he who *knows* he knows and knows what he does not know. As with everyone else, there are some things for which you are expert and other things you can only dream of doing well. We are all faced with this. No one is ever really qualified for the next promotion, yet most take it because of the challenge. On the other hand, most of us are not experts at everything. We need help. Sometimes there is more help within the organization than we realize. You should discuss your thoughts with others. Speak to your senior finance and human resources people. Talk with your immediate staff. Who should do what in carrying out changes? Does the organization need to look for outside help?

ACTIONS SPEAK LOUDER THAN WORDS

Perhaps the most important advice is: do *something*. Plan your actions, but do not plan forever. Decide what to do, how and who should do it, and get on with it!

Do not let the quest for perfection inhibit you from doing good.

Notes

Chapter 1

1. ANSI/ISO/ASQ Q9000-2000, *Quality Management Systems—Fundamentals and Vocabulary*, Milwaukee: ASQ, 2000.
2. ANSI/ISO/ASQ Q9004-2000, *Quality Management Systems—Guidelines for Performance Improvements*, Milwaukee: ASQ, 2000.
3. ANSI/ISO/ASQ Q9001-2000, *Quality Management Systems—Requirements*, Milwaukee: ASQ, 2000.
4. http://www.iso.org/iso/en/iso9000-14000/iso9000/qmp.html. Document on "Quality Management Principles," accessed 5 June 2001 and 17 June 2004.
5. http://www.EFQM.org. Article on EFQM Excellence Model, "Model Refreshing Project Summary of Changes," accessed 12 December 2002.
6. http://www.efqm.org/model_awards/model/excellence_model.htm, accessed 17 June 2004.
7. http://www.efqm.org/downloads, accessed 17 June 2004.
8. http://www.quality.nist.gov/Criteria.htm, accessed 17 June 2004.
9. Japanese Standards Association, Tokyo, 2003. For inquiries contact Industry Science and Technology Policy and Environment Bureau, Conformity Assessment Division, Ministry of Economy, Trade and Industry, 3-1 Kasumigaseke 1-Chome, Chiyoda-ku, Tokyo 100-8901, Japan.
10. Myers, David G., *Intuition, Its Powers and Perils*, New Haven, CT: Yale University Press, 2002.

Chapter 2

1. Caplan, R. S., and D. P. Norton, *The Balanced Scorecard,* Boston, MA: Harvard Business School Press, 1996.
2. Deming, W. Edwards, *Out of the Crisis,* Cambridge, MA: Center for Advanced Engineering Study, 1988.
3. Goodman, John A., and Steve Newman, "Six Steps to Integrating Complaint Data into Decisions," *Quality Progress,* February 2003, p. 42.
4. Vavra, Terry F., *Customer Satisfaction Measurement Simplified,* Milwaukee: ASQ Quality Press, 2002, p. 13.
5. Campanella, Jack, ed., *Principles of Quality Costs,* Milwaukee: ASQ Quality Press, 1999.

Chapter 3

1. Goodman, John A., and Steve Newman, "Six Steps to Integrating Complaint Data into QA Decisions," *Quality Progress,* February 2003, p. 43.
2. Treachy, M., *Double-Digit Growth,* New York: Portfolio, 2003.
3. Hotel example comes from videotape *Quality Is Your Job,* John E. (Jack) West and Charles A. Cianfrani, Durham, NC: Inform, 2004. Used with permission.
4. Saunders, D. M., Charles A. Cianfrani, and Wayne G. Robertshaw, *Measurement of Customer Satisfaction*, ASQ ISO 9000:2000 Handbook, Chapter 29, ed. by Charles A. Cianfrani, John E. (Jack) West, and Joseph J. Tsiakals, Milwaukee: ASQ Quality Press, 2002.

Chapter 4

1. Senge, Peter M., *The Fifth Discipline,* New York: Doubleday/Currency, 1990, pp. 218–222.

Chapter 5

1. Senge, Peter M., *The Fifth Discipline,* New York: Doubleday/Currency, 1990, p. 68.
2. Senge, pp. 57–67.
3. Senge, p. 69.
4. Senge, p. 72.
5. Galloway, Dianne, *Mapping Work Processes,* Milwaukee: ASQ Quality Press, 1994; Tague, Nancy R., *The Quality Toolbox,* Milwaukee: ASQ Quality Press, 1995; and Escoe, Adrienne, *The Practical Guide to People Friendly Documentation*, Milwaukee: ASQ Quality Press, 2001.
6. Tapping, Don, Tom Luyster, and Tom Shuker, *Value Stream Management: Eight Steps to Planning, Mapping, and Sustaining Lean Improvements*, New York: Productivity Press, 2002, p. 78.
7. Camp, Robert C., *Benchmarking, The Search for Industry Best Practices that Lead to Superior Performance*, Milwaukee: ASQ Quality Press, 1989.
8. Hammar, M., and J. Champy, *Reengineering the Corporation,* New York: Harper, 1993.
9. Thomas, D. W., Chairman, Handbook Committee, *Statistical Quality Control Handbook,* AT&T, Western Electric, 1956, 1958 2nd ed., 11th printing, Charlotte, NC: Delmar, 1985; and Barrentine, Larry, *An Introduction to Design of Experiments: A Simplified Approach,* Milwaukee: ASQ Quality Press, 1999.
10. O'Connor, Patrick D. T., *Practical Reliability Engineering*, Chichester, UK: John Wiley and Sons, Wiley Haden Limited, 1983.
11. Palmer, Brien, *Making Change Work: Practical Tools for Overcoming Human Resistance to Change,* Milwaukee: ASQ Quality Press, 2003, p. 7.

Chapter 6

1. These concepts were introduced many years ago by Dr. J. M. Juran.
2. Godfrey, A. Blanton, "Problem Solved, Now What?" *Quality Digest,* March 2004, p. 16.

Chapter 7

1. Tague, Nancy R., *The Quality Toolbox,* Milwaukee: ASQ Quality Press, 1995.
2. For a service process example, see Cianfrani, Charles A., and West, John E. (Jack), *Cracking the Case of ISO 9001:2000 for Service,* Milwaukee: ASQ Quality Press, 2003, Tool 8—Failure Mode and Effects Analysis, pp. 166–169. For a manufacturing example, see Cianfrani, Charles A., and West, John E. (Jack), *Cracking the Case of ISO 9001:2000 for Manufacturing,* Milwaukee: ASQ Quality Press, 2003, Tool 8—Failure Mode and Effects Analysis, pp. 166–169.
3. Glefick, James, *Chaos, Making a New Science,* New York: Viking Penguin, 1987.
4. Deming, W. Edwards, *Out of the Crisis,* Cambridge, MA: Center for Advanced Engineering Study, 1989.
5. McGill, Bruce K., "Return to Chaos," *Quality Progress,* November 1990, 55–57
6. DeMeyer, Arnould, Christoph H. Loch, and Michael T. Pich, "Managing Project Uncertainty: from Variation to Chaos," *MIT Sloan Management Review,* Winter 2002, p. 60.

Chapter 8

1. Arter, Dennis R., Charles A. Cianfrani, and John E. (Jack) West, *How to Audit the Process-Based QMS,* Milwaukee: ASQ Quality Press, 2003.

Chapter 9

1. http://www.quality.nist.gov/Criteria.htm, "Criteria for Performance Excellence; Baldrige National Quality Program," accessed 17 June 2004.
2. Japanese Standards Association, Tokyo, 2003; for inquiries contact Industry Science and Technology Policy and Environment Bureau, Conformity Assessment Division, Ministry of Economy, Trade and Industry, 3-1 Kasumigaseke 1-Chome, Chiyoda-ku, Tokyo 100-8901, Japan, JIS TR Q0005 QMS Guidelines for sustainable growth; and Japanese Standards Association, Tokyo, 2003; for inquiries contact Industry Science and Technology Policy and Environment Bureau, Conformity Assessment Division, Ministry of Economy, Trade and Industry, 3-1 Kasumigaseke 1-Chome, Chiyoda-ku, Tokyo 100-8901, Japan, JIS TR Q0006 QMS Guidelines for self-assessment.

Chapter 10

1. *Business 2.0,* vol. 5, no. 4, May 2004, p. 101.
2. Palmer, Brien, *Making Change Work: Practical Tools for Overcoming Human Resistance to Change,* Milwaukee: ASQ Quality Press, 2003.

Index